GOOD COMPANY

TIM MILES

To order additional copies, visit OurIAG.com or call 855-503-0677.

Cover design by Laura Harris, Jessica Kohler, and Tim Miles
Author Photograph Handled by Rhiannon Trask
Author Neuroses Handled by Deidre Miles and Lynn Peisker

Copyright © 2012 TIM MILES & IAG PRESS

ISBN-13: 978-0615665115 (IAG Press)
ISBN-10: 061566511X
LCCN: 2012943679

For Bubs and Choo Choo and Their Most Amazing Mama

*The goal of life is to take everything
that made you weird as a kid and
get people to pay you money
for it as an adult.*
~ David Freeman

CONTENTS

KEEPING GOOD COMPANY

BEING GOOD COMPANY

ACKNOWLEDGMENTS

I'm wildly and profoundly flawed. Thanks, first, to God for helping me in every way.

Thanks to Roy and Pennie Williams for never giving up.

Thanks to our clients for patience, courage and faith - most notably my neighbors in all this, the Chapman family.

Thanks to my partners in Wizard of Ads - most notably my neighbor in all this, Paul Boomer.

Thanks to everyone who contributed to the book - including Boomer, Lynn, Ryan, Jeff, Bryan, Peter, and, of course, Roy.

Thanks to my parents, Rich and Janet Miles, and my whole family, for allowing me to grow up healthy, happy and curious while surrounded by books and tractors.

Special thanks to my two big sisters, Lynn Peisker and Michele Miller, for encouragement and butt-kicking.

Thanks to Scotty for teaching me everything I know ... right?

Thanks to David, Meghan and Will for letting me hog a table in the back to write most of this book at D. Rowe's.

Thanks to Julie Patrick for editing ... and for saying "yes" to Ryan.

Thanks to Ryan Patrick for twenty years of everything.

Lastly, thanks to Bill & Penny Ottesen for raising four amazing, hard-working, smart and occasionally stubborn daughters. I can't believe the third one said, "I do." I'd be a fraction of the man I am today without her.

FOREWORD

There's a cheap kind of success that looks the part but can't quite swing the hammer. This cheap success is common among advertising consultants. You've seen it, I'm sure; an expensive suit, twinkling eyes, perfect teeth, a Rolex and a $100 haircut. Lots of name dropping.

Tim's success was never cheap.

Tim can swing the hammer.

I invited Tim Miles to become my business partner after he had attended a few of my classes. You can tell a lot about a person when you grade their homework. Tim's homework showed none of the tendencies common to young ad writers. Tim's work reflected the wisdom of experience.

Young advertising professionals learn bitter lessons. The first of these lessons is that clever ideas don't always work. When a man has a conscience, there is no better teacher than Failure. But you cannot meet this teacher until you've been given the opportunity to play the game of Marketing with real companies, real dollars, real responsibility.

As a criminally overworked ad writer for a group of radio stations with hundreds of clients, Tim Miles was crafting more campaigns every month than a Madison Avenue ad man will create in his entire career. This is not an exaggeration.

Think of it: hundreds of small companies running the ads you write for them, then reporting their results to you, month after month, year after year. Can you imagine a more perfect laboratory? Could there be a better classroom? In terms of real-world experience, Tim was 200 years old before he was 30.

All *Wizard of Ads* partners are given annual raises based on the growth of their clients. When I told Tim how much he could expect to make as my partner, his eyes widened appreciably. The amount I mentioned was about five times the salary he had made the previous year. Today Tim earns nearly four times what I promised him that day. Not because he charges a lot of money, but because his clients have grown and grown and grown.

And then grown some more.

Tim gets annual raises from happy clients who are delighted with the success he has helped them achieve.

And now he is going to help you. With simple ideas, plain-spoken truth, the wisdom of experience.

Relax, you're in good company.

Roy H. Williams,
Tim's partner and the author of the
New York Times and *Wall Street Journal*
bestselling **Wizard of Ads** trilogy

PREFACE

The system we grew up in is a mess. It's falling apart at the seams and a lot of people I care about are in pain because the things we thought would work don't.
~ Seth Godin

Fish don't know they're in water. You've been like that, too.

Tried-and-trusted methods of communication no longer ring true in today's marketplace.

What's more (or less, as the case may be), the systems you relied upon are failing ... maybe.

If you want to not only survive but thrive in this century, you're going to need to reorient yourself to a new way of thinking.

Inside this book, you'll find three sections devoted to case studies, lessons learned, and tried-and-true stories of business growth, customer delight and personal development.

In "Making Good Company," you'll learn about strategy and about what matters and what doesn't to consumers today. You'll learn to critically and objectively analyze what you're trying to make happen, and what's in your way.

In "Keeping Good Company," you'll learn some of the secrets that have helped my words win customers in seven countries. You'll see and - through a complementary private website - hear actual examples of copywriting and customer service success stories to help you win new customers and delight the ones you already have.

In "Being Good Company," you'll learn some techniques for separating the truly important from the merely urgent. You'll take a look inside the Miles family - where Dee and I have learned to look at the world a little differently since our son was diagnosed with autism.

A book filled with heart, humor and historical success, *Good Company* will help you live, work and play a little better, a little truer, and a little stronger.

If you're looking for a quick fix, you're going to come away disappointed.

This book is the diet and exercise of marketing and communication and persuasion. If you're looking for a bag of magic beans, I wish you the best of luck. But don't worry – I'm sure some social media expert will be along in a few minutes.

For those who are willing to do the work, I invite you to pass here, and go on.

You are on the road to heaven.

TIM MILES

MAKING

I. THE FIRST LESSON

"Tim, I think Will has autism."

Six little words. The day everything changed. November 21, 2005. Our son, Will, had just turned thirteen months old the day before - when all was right with the world.

Less than thirty days before, I'd quit my job. In just under eighteen months, I'd built a million dollar company for someone else, and - with the help of some wizards - wanted to see if I could do the same for my family.

We could have - and maybe should have - punted right there and then. I could have begged for my job back ... or, as some suggested, gone to work at Best Buy.

Instead - we went forward fiercely - lost at first, but relentless.

And since then, we've built a company of our own, raised a child with special needs and watched him bloom, and also had a daughter who suffers from a terrible affliction known as melodrama.

Above all, we survived. We endured.

According to Autism Speaks, eight out of every ten marriages of parents of a child with autism end in divorce. Oof.

Our faith in God and our faith in each other have grown.

Our business has grown.

Our wealth, health and happiness have all improved - in spite of the fact we've never been busier.

How?

Because of a lesson taught to me by Will's first therapists. It's a lesson you simply must understand before we can continue.

Parts of this book will be uncomfortable. Parts of this book will be hard work. Parts of this book will be relentless.

If you're looking for the magic bullet book, boy, did you pick up the wrong one.

This one's the diet and exercise of work and life and play and hope.

The signs are easy to read. The stories - at least, all but one - are true. The steps to take are simple.

It doesn't mean they're easy.

The first step? The first lesson taught to us by Will's very first therapists - when we were lost and sad and angry and still certainly very much in shock?

You cannot expect someone else to change his behavior until you're first willing to change your own.

Indirectly, it was Will's first lesson for us. It wouldn't be his last.

Thanks, buddy.

2. A SIGN OF THINGS TO COME

Do me favor. Grab a sheet of paper and a pen. I'll wait.

Now - sign your name.

(Turn the page.)

Now. Switch hands and do it again.

I love doing this exercise at the beginning of workshops and little talks I give from time to time because it's such a clear illustration of the awkward discomfort we're about to experience together.

Change is awkward.

Change doesn't feel right - those bad habits have carved out well-rutted neuro-pathways and have no interest in climbing out of them.

But you must.

If I whacked your dominant hand with a hammer, then duct-taped it behind your back for six weeks, sure, it might smell a little after a while, but what a change would take place to your weaker hand!

We're going to stretch, struggle and reach for something new today.

And tomorrow, it'll feel a little less awkward.

This, today, I pledge to you.

3. LISTEN CLOSELY NOW.
THIS IS IMPORTANT.

Okay, while you've got pen and paper handy, I want you to do me another favor.

List out all your business' competitors. Take your time. Don't rush.

I'll wait ... give yourself a little longer ... make sure you have everybody.

Got 'em? Now, count 'em up.

How many do you have?

Wow. A bunch, huh?

Okay, now one more favor, and then you can sit back and read for a while.

List all the major brands of hearing aids. Take your time. Don't rush.

I'll wait ... give yourself a little longer ... make sure you have everybody.

Got 'em? Now, count 'em up.

How many do you have?

Wow. Two, huh?*

Listen carefully: To everyone else, your business category is no different than hearing aids.

People can maybe name one or two in your market in your business category.

Are you one of them? Which one? And what feelings do people associate with your name? Do you know?

Does it bother you that you don't know?

About a billion times, I've had business owners preach to me about the fact that *if consumers only knew this and that and the other about this industry, they'd surely pick us because, dangit, we're the best.*

Of course you are, but no one cares. No one has the time. There's simply too much noise and most of it sounds like that irritating squeal that rang from Grandma June's Beltone in 1986.

Squeeeeeeeeeeee ... that's everybody but maybe the top one or two in your business category.

Would you like to know how to begin to tune in? We'll talk about it throughout this book.

I hope you're listening.

* Most people get either Beltone or Miracle Ear or both. In all the years of doing this business, I've never had anyone - outside the occasional wearer or retailer - name three. There are 16 brands.

4. OPPORTUNITY? IT COSTS.

You can't have everything. Where would you put it?
~ Steven Wright

What are you willing to give up?

Are you willing to repel a couple people to gain one for life?

Are you willing to make a choice and head down a path at the expense of others?

You'd better be.

If you fail, try something else.

One of my clients' keys to success invariably seems to be that they're willing to take action and do stuff.

All opportunities cost. The cost might be time. It might be money. It might be waving goodbye to another road.

In your company, what are you willing to give up?

For example, in your advertising or your systems or policies or procedures, are you willing to absolutely repel someone to gain one for life?

Are you willing to so strongly attract someone through your beliefs that you risk of repelling someone else just as strongly?

Are you willing to have a few people hate your advertising and tell you so?

What are you prepared to do?

What are you prepared to give up to gain something else?

We can't do everything. We can't be all things to all people - nor do we want to be.

Are you willing to put your head down, make a choice and move forward step-by-step down one path at the expense of other paths and opportunities?

You'd better be.

And if you fail, try something else.

Don't whine and complain. I often tell people that my clients succeed for really three reasons:

1. **They're people of action. They do things. They're willing to, as my partner Roy H. Williams says, pull the trigger and ride the bullet.**

We try things. We take action. We swing the hammer. As I get older raw talent impresses me less and less, and relentlessness impresses me more and more.

Are you dedicated to becoming a success? Dedication requires sacrifice. Sacrifice is another way of saying "opportunity costs."

2. **The second key to success I've seen time and time again as a defining characteristic of all of my clients: They are very good at what they do, and they love talking about what they do.**

There may be no more boring topic on the face of the planet than roofing.

Unless you are Patrick Morin of Roof Life of Oregon in Portland. Listen to Patrick talk with passion and authenticity about how important it is that your roof be safe so your family will be safe. Listen to him go into detail about how Portland gets ten feet of rain every year pounding on those nails, on the shingles, on the shakes, and how with just simple preventive maintenance you could keep so many expensive problems from occurring.

As he talks, he waves his arms and his eyebrows leap eight inches off his head. He will make you a roofing zealot, I promise you. He can also save you thousands of dollars in repairs if you listen to him.

"Patrick, is that a tear in your eye?"

Can you be that passionate about your company? If not, it's probably time to change companies.

3. **The third secret? Sorry - we reserve that one for our clients. :)**

5. TURNING PRO

One of my heroes, Steven Pressfield, from one of the three most important books in my life:

The moment an artist turns pro is as epochal as the birth of his first child. With one stroke, everything changes. I can state absolutely that the term of my life can be divided into two parts: before turning pro, and after.

To be clear: When I say professional, I don't mean doctors and lawyers, those of "the professions." I mean the Professional as an ideal. The professional in contrast to the amateur. Consider the differences.

The amateur plays for fun. The professional plays for keeps.

To the amateur, the game is his avocation. To the pro it's his vocation.

The amateur plays part-time, the professional full-time.

The amateur is a weekend warrior. The professional is there seven days a week.

The word amateur comes from the Latin root meaning "to love." The conventional interpretation is that the amateur pursues his calling out of love, while the pro does it for money. Not the way I see it. In my view, the amateur does not love the game enough. If he did, he would not pursue it as a sideline, distinct from his "real" vocation.

The professional loves it so much he dedicates his life to it. He commits full-time.

That's what I mean when I say turning pro.[1]

Are you ready to turn pro, too?

Best I can tell, there are a few other things professionals require:

Professionals listen more than they talk.

Even then, professionals often let their actions do the talking.

Professionals are almost boring in their consistency and dependability.

Professionals know they can't do it alone – they need lawyers, bankers, accountants, designers, printers, rodeo clowns and other professionals.

Professionals act exactly the same when no one's looking.

Professionals get clarity up front.

Professionals finish. They deliver. They follow-through … and they do all these things even when they're not feeling up to it … especially then.

[1]*Pressfield, Steven (2002-06-01). THE WAR OF ART (pp. 62-63). Rugged Land. Kindle Edition.*

6. STRATEGIC PLANNING - IT'S ELEMENTARY

(Bragging Father's Note: It's worth pointing out that our son was non-verbal just a couple years ago. We never cease to be awed by his progress, his mind, and the patient guidance he receives from his teachers, therapists, and classmates.)

The morning after I'd gotten back from speaking to a group of not-for-profit organizations, Will said to me:

"Daddy, you should come speak to my class."

"Will, what should I talk about?"

"I don't know. Rachel's mom talked about Hanukkah. Do you want to talk about Hanukkah?"

"Probably not, buddy."

"Okay. You think about it."

So I did.

Listen, I've spoken on a stage in front of more than a thousand people, and it didn't produce more than a flutter of anxiety, but at that moment – trying to imagine holding the interest of a group of forty discerning elementary school students – I nearly soiled one of Baby Sarah's diapers.

How could I engage them?

Well, with storytelling, I suppose. It's kinda what I do.

So I thought about every Pixar movie we love and deconstructed a simple, foolproof method for inventing any story that I could then teach to the children.

I think. It's seemed foolproof. It worked on my son. But – I don't know if I've mentioned this – he's alarmingly and unfairly intelligent. And handsome.

Daddy's Fool-proof, Sure-fire, Rock-solid, Lots-of-hyphens Storytelling Formula

Answer these questions:

1. Who's your story about?

2. Is anybody with them? Who?

3. Where are they going?

4. Why?

5. Is there a bad guy?

6. Who?

7. What's in their way?

8. Why?

9. How do they get around it?

10. How do they live happily ever after?

Go ahead, try it. Tell me you couldn't write a great story following that formula.

Oh, and tell me also – isn't that pretty much strategic planning? Couldn't you use it to simplify the problems facing your business? Try it the next time your worries get too big.

7. HOW TO WORK ON STUFF THAT MATTERS

BIG ROCKS
Week of: August 22

1. Finish Pass Website
2. Work on PARC Mktg. Campaign
3. Create Master Spreadsheet of Client Work
4. Finish Initial Strategy for Greiner
5. Finish Initial Strategy for Lavine's
6. Finish Executive Summary of Book - send to MM

The Week's Big Rocks

While on vacation in Scotland and Ireland, I spent some time re-reading the book that helped me get turned around a couple years ago in terms of focus and productivity – working on stuff that matters versus being a slave to my inbox and other people's agendas instead of my own.

Leo Babauta wrote *Zen To Done* because he couldn't find a perfect system to help him accomplish the work that mattered to him. He took bits and pieces of different methodologies, which he credits fully in his e-book.

In the past couple weeks, in spite of being in twenty-five airports in forty-five days, we worked really hard to get caught up, and I'd not only like to stay that way, but to step even harder on the gas to move even further into pro-activity with our business.

One of my favorite exercises from the book was – on Sunday evening or Monday morning – establish the week's "big rocks" (a term the author got from Steven Covey) – those things that are most important to accomplish in the week ahead. This helps you not fall victim to the constant drum of urgency from the inbox.

You shouldn't list more than a half-dozen or so. Hopefully, at least one of them relates to your larger goals. Schedule them now.

I'm going to print and post this weekly list on my monitor or in my hotel room if I'm traveling.

Then, each day – choose your three most important tasks for the day and schedule time to work on them.

These three tasks will – at some point – include your week's big rocks. That way, by week's end, all your most important tasks will be finished.

Try and get each day's most important tasks done early – when you have the most energy.

When you're working on them, close your email and turn off your phone.

Finish one. Take a break. Start on another.

When I was doing this regularly, I'd never been more productive. I'd never felt better. Over time, I fell away from it.

I've just recently started again. If you're struggling with separating the truly important from the merely urgent, why not try it with me?

Send your weekly list to someone who will help hold you accountable (not me) – like I do with Dee and Ryan.

Even though our business has grown by fifty percent this year, this system scales perfectly to help you get the important stuff done.

8. HOW TO HAVE A BETTER WEEKEND

Before you call it a weekend, tie up a loose end.

Or grab the scissors and cut it off.

Fix something that needs fixed.

That monotonous little project that you've been pushing back from one day to the next on your to-do list for days/weeks/months?

Do it.

You know which one I'm talking about. Give yourself permission to get closure.

Lighten your mental load.

That call you haven't made? Make it.

That thing you haven't written? Write it.

That noun you haven't verbed? Verb it.

Give your mental health that gift before you call it a weekend.

Do it. Before noon, please.

I'll do the same.

9. UNHAPPY AT WORK?

For reasons I can't quite explain, in the last couple of months, I have recently been discreetly contacted by no less than ten people who are dissatisfied with their current stations in life. Two of them work for the same company!

They've all wondered if I knew of something better or something new.

These are not nose-pickers, mind you. Every one of the no-less-than-ten is smart, dependable and talented.

I don't know whether this is, in fact, a pattern or trend, but it is interesting, isn't it?

I don't recommend or refer easily – I've been hurt before, you know.

But I know five things – the first from my mentor, Mike Reis:

1. **"It's easier to get a job when you have a job."**

Remember that. Don't be hasty. Don't make ultimatums where you're not prepared to accept either outcome. Don't back bosses into corners.

Bosses bite sometimes.

Here's some more advice for you if you're currently dissatisfied:

2. **Understand your cost of staying power** – that's a term I learned from Roy. Staying power's what you need to pay your monthly bills and have a little blow money. You know

Dave Ramsey's stuff? It's like his basic spreadsheet. You don't need to live like a monk, but you do need to know this number. I don't care what you want to make. I don't care what you think you deserve to make. I care about staying power, and you should, too. The lower that number, the more freedom you have to take risks and explore options.

3. Keep your profile/resume updated. If you're not on LinkedIn, you need to be, and your profile needs to be updated. Asking for recommendations doesn't hurt either.

4. Speaking of the online world, Google yourself. It's an easy way to do a superficial background check on you. Is your Facebook page public? Are there pictures of you doing body shots or dressing up like Hitler? You might want to consider Googling yourself – your future employers will.

But, this is maybe the most important question to ask yourself:

5. Will a new job solve your problem? Or is it something else?

Sometimes it really is the job – whether it's a toxic environment or unchallenging position or no chance for professional growth.

But even if it is the job, how do you get from the beginning to the end of the day without having a drink until you find something new?

Get your sugar out of a different bowl.

Get a hobby. Invest your time, talent and heart into a passion that has nothing to do with work.

Volunteer. Garden. Learn Mandarin.

Exorcise the office demon. Don't let it bring you down (as well as those around you). Remember to remain positive at work – in spite of everything you may feel about the place, don't drag others down. Plus, whining and feeling sorry for yourself and wearing your misery mask and cape just make the days go by more slowly.

Get your sugar out of a different bowl.

You may even learn it's not so bad. At least, for awhile.

10. WANT TO

We might need to have a difficult conversation.

I write a lot about motivation and productivity. I get a lot of questions about those subjects, so I keep thinking about them.

And I think there's a hard realization some people need to face.

Maybe – deep down in your secret world – *you just don't want to do it.*

Maybe you don't want to spend more time with your family.

Maybe you don't want to lose the weight or write the book or change the world.

Or change your world.

Oh, sure, maybe you like *the idea* of being it – whatever *it* is. It might be being happily married or being in shape or being a best-selling author.

But, dude, being and doing are two waaaaaaay different things.

Get out of denial. Admit it. Then work on *that* instead of pretending to go through the motions half-heartedly flailing at this other thing.

Maybe this other thing is too hard. Maybe this other thing is too much work or will take too much time. Maybe, today, you're just not willing to really and truly make the effort.

And it's not for me or anyone else to decide whether or not that's okay.

But you need to admit it to yourself ... so you can stop living the lie.

You'll be happier, or you'll know it's time to make a change.

It's kinda like the old saying:

When you're torn between two things, flip a coin. You don't flip it to see where it lands. You flip it because – while it's still in the air – your heart will tell you which way you really want the coin to fall.

Got a quarter?

(If this totally doesn't apply to you, awesome. But I bet – like me – *somebody* popped into your head. Should we do something about it? What do you think? I don't know, either. I'm just asking.)

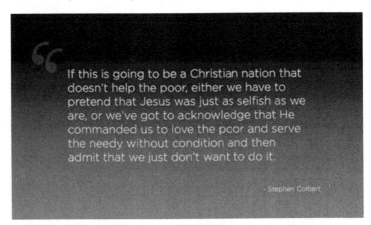

If this is going to be a Christian nation that doesn't help the poor, either we have to pretend that Jesus was just as selfish as we are, or we've got to acknowledge that He commanded us to love the poor and serve the needy without condition and then admit that we just don't want to do it.

- Stephen Colbert

II. TITHE

I started my advertising career in 1995 for a country radio station in southern Illinois. I made $305.42 every two weeks. I would frequently pull the acoustical tiles off the wall, lay them on the floor and sleep on them for a few hours before getting back to work. You couldn't pry me out of that place - a converted Mexican restaurant.

Even then, I vowed to spend ten percent of my meager earnings on improving my career.

Books, audio seminars, lessons, conferences.

Yeah, my own money.

Yeah, it hurt. Growing usually does.

Best decision I ever made. I tell it to college and high school classes whenever I get the chance.

I still do it today.

Tithe to your career.

But sleep in a bed.

Trust me on this one.

12. PULL BACK THE COVERS

Walking on water wasn't built in a day.
~ Jack Kerouac

Inertia rocks.

You know what doesn't?

"I'll start tomorrow."

All you need is will and a catalyst (and perhaps, if you're really lucky, a partner like my wife to provide you with honest-to-goodness inspiration).

For me, the catalyst is pulling back the covers at 4:30 AM. If I can get the covers pulled back and free myself from the cocoon, I can get up the stairs.

What's the next simple step?

If I can get the desk lamp on my office turned on, I can sit down.

What's the next simple step?

If I can get the to-do list opened, I can start on the first task.

Inertia.

It's just so easy for us to say we'll do it later.

What isn't easy is doing it later.

What's your next simple step?

Do it. Now. I'll wait … … …

It's now 5:44 AM. After some quiet, inspirational moments of conversation with my wife, Dee, I've been working for nearly an hour.

Do you know how good that feels?

13. "I WANT TO DO WHAT YOU DO."

I hear this a lot.

I'll hear it at least a half-dozen times next week when Dee and I visit San Antonio for the International Water Quality Association convention to deliver the opening keynote address.

Dee says it's because sometimes I make it look too easy, so it makes others feel like they can quite naturally get on stage in front of a thousand people, too, and speak from their hearts about their *passions*.

And no one will throw fruit.

You want to do what I do?

Okay.

Get up earlier than you want. Not just tomorrow but for years.

Read for about two hours a day. Not just blogs but books and not just business books, but book books.

Especially book books.

Turn off your television and keep it off.

Take an acting class. Then take them for ten years or so. You'll be terrible at first, and it'll be the most awful hot feeling in your face you've ever felt. You'll lie awake nights recounting your profound ability to suck.

But it'll get better. Slowly.

Write.

Write every day. Write when you don't feel like it.

Especially when you don't feel like it.

Find someone who will read the stuff you wrote and talk to them.

Tell 'em some more stuff. They won't pay you any money for this.

You probably won't get paid money for a couple years.

But, if you have something to say, and you say it interestingly enough, not only will the audience not throw fruit, but someone in the audience will know another group who would like to hear you speak or a business that would be willing to pay you a little bit of money to help them.

Be prepared to lie awake at night knowing the infinitesimally remote possibility that every one of your clients could fire you tomorrow is still a possibility. This especially happens alone in the countless, nameless hotel rooms you'll come to call home way more than you'd like.

Do your best to ignore the trolls, gutter snipes and booger eaters who'll do their best to dismiss you, steal your stuff and stab you in the back.

But, also be ready to admit you're doing the best you can and, thank God, you're curious enough and determined enough (and possibly stupid enough) to never give up the dream of doing this.

Whatever *this* is ...

Be prepared to have awkward conversations on airplanes and in queues and even at parties with your friends about what it is you do, exactly.

Oh, and you'll have this conversation with your mother, too.

Repeatedly.

And don't whine or complain or makes excuses, okay? No one's asking you to grab a rifle and man a post.

And it's all worth it. I think – to do what it is I do.

After all, I'm writing this in my underwear, wearing unconscionably nice headphones, and I was able to long ago move out of my parents' proverbial basement.

I do get to spend a nice week in San Antonio with my wife and two of my best buddies. That part's cool.

We're able to provide every possible opportunity and resource for our special needs child.

You just try to focus on doing the next right thing.

But it all started with getting up early and reading and writing and reading some more and then doing.

It's a long way to the stage.

But, most days, the view's pretty good from up there.

I hope I get to watch you someday.

I promise I won't throw fruit.

14. BLIND SPOTS AND UNCOMFORTABLE POSITIONS

"Our competition copies everything we do. No kidding. Our newspaper ads. Our Yellow Pages. We even changed our logo, and they changed theirs."

This is what one of my clients told me in our first visit together. A mid-western heating and air conditioning company – they'd been referred to me by another one of my clients.

They had been down or flat for a few years. This was 2008.

Within a few hours, I had diagnosed the problem.

You see, they were already good at what they did. Very good. The owner was an expert among experts. *He was so good that he taught heating and air conditioning classes at the local technical college.*

And Dr. Comfort was born. And so began a brand and a strategy all built around being the smartest, the most highly-trained and the one who best understands higher degrees of comfort.

He'd been teaching there for years, but he never thought it was relevant. He didn't think customers would care. Turns out, they did. A lot.

In a recent *Monday Morning Memo*, Roy wrote:

Every business owner has a blind spot. Do you know yours?

That was a trick question. Of course you don't know your blind spot. If you knew it was there, it wouldn't be a blind spot.

When a business owner can't figure out how to take his company to the next level, it's usually because the stairway that will take him there is hiding behind his blind spot.

You can't see your own blind spot because you're on the inside, looking out. The first step of a good consultant is to be a friendly pair of eyes on the outside, looking in.

A friendly pair of eyes to help you evaluate your limiting factors.

A friendly pair of eyes to help you find the message you must shout to the world.

A friendly pair of eyes to show you the opportunity that hides behind your blind spot.

I'm very proud of my Wizard of Ads partners. They're doing a lot of good for a lot of people.

Now, I'm sure those competitors think we're nuts – running on the radio like darned fools – week after week – with no specials or price discounts. Why, we're not even mentioning the brands we sell. Yep. Nuts.

Double-digit-growth nuts.

Year-after-year nuts.

Voted-Contractor-of-the-Year-by-their-peers-last-month nuts.

We need a Doctor.

15. THE GREEN VEGETABLES OF WORK

My friend Megan asked:

What tips do you have in prioritizing work, keeping a good to-do list, staying organized, and getting it all done in forty hours a week?

Okay. Here's how I do it. (Written with help from my Organizational Yoda: Deidre Miles)

FOCUS

Only check email and voicemail three times a day. Don't let other people's unscheduled interruptions deter you from your day. I have one private email address and one way to reach me in case of emergency. Everything else is vetted by someone better at it than me.

Only process stuff a couple times a day ... and when you do, actually process it. Actionable items from email – get them on your to-do list. Items that someone else has to do – get 'em off your back and onto theirs, scheduling only a follow-up reminder to make sure they've done the work.

Need to send emails? Fine. No problem. Just don't *check* any other emails. Does this require discipline? Absolutely. If it was easy, everybody would be doing it. This is at the top of my email signature:

*** PLEASE NOTE: I have begun checking email only three times per day to be more valuable to my clients, partners and family. If it's an emergency, please call. ***

That call would go to our amazing virtual receptionists at www.callruby.com that know how to find me or find those who can reach me.

What about during-the-day ideas? Ideas for ads or blog posts or gifts for others? Capture it. Send yourself a quick email if you can do it without checking other emails. Shoot yourself a text. Write it down in a notebook. But process it all later during the next time you process.

Put these email/voicemail-processing times on your calendar. The most important thing you have to do each day? That goes on the calendar, too. Maybe two things. No more than three important things on your calendar each day. Hopefully, one of those important things moves you toward some greater goal – even if it's just a tiny step, make it. Just keep moving toward your big, hairy goal.

Okay, you've got your list. You've got it processed.

Now, before you start, review and prioritize the list. Are there monkeys that really shouldn't be on *your* back? Delegate them right now. Quickly – what else can you say "no, thank you" to? Don't be the bottleneck.

Got it? Ready? Go.

DO THE WORK

Close out the world and get to work.

Work the list. Go Pac-Man on that list.

Believe it or not, I actually have a light-switch I throw in my mind's eye.

When your mind starts to wander. When the phone rings (if you forgot to shut it off). When Twitter tweets (if you forgot to shut it off). When Stars Dance.

Get back to the list.

Schedule what really matters. Every morning, pay yourself first. Drink another glass of water. Don't eat crap. Energy counts. If you need to take a ten-minute break, set a timer and take a break.

Then, honor the timer. Get back to the list.

MEETINGS

Try your darnedest to schedule meetings (including calls) during your *least* productive time. I'm more productive, creative and effective in the morning. Therefore, I try to schedule meetings in the afternoon – and back to back if possible. It's harder to re-groove after one meeting when you know you've only got an hour before the next one.

I also try to schedule all my meetings only on a couple chosen days of the week. That way I'm left with a few non-meeting days with less interruptions to focus on being productive.

If you have a meeting, make sure there's an agenda in advance. Stick to the agenda. No meeting ends without action items, assignments and deadlines. If a meeting ends without those, congratulations – the meeting organizer just wasted everyone's time.

So, the meeting ends? Get back to your workplace and work.

BE RELENTLESS

Get back to the list.

When you start to doubt the work ... others ... yourself ...

Get back to the list. This is not the time for reflection. This is the time for work.

When it's time to add something to the list, add it. Capture it. Get it out of your head. Get it out of there! Whatever – blog idea – ad idea – to make room for more stuff.

Then get back to work.

Work the list. Work. The. List.

End each day by reviewing your progress and setting the table for the next day.

THAT'S IT

It's not sexy. Sorry. This is the green vegetable stuff. It's good for you and gives you more energy than you ever thought possible ... even if candy's sweeter and more fun.

(By the way, I used to be addicted to productivity app switching. I thought the app made a big difference. It doesn't – whether it costs $150 or is a piece of scratch paper. Pick one. Stick with it. Do the work.)

Additional Reading: Before you get back to work, check out Henry Miller's *11 Commandments of Writing & Daily Creative Routine.*

You can find a link at www.GoodCompanyStuff.com.

PS: Organizational Yoda would make a great band name.

16. WHAT IF YOU WERE WORTH $300 AN HOUR?

I wanted to share something with you that's already made an incalculable difference in my life, and I hope it'll make you think.

Last year, I decided my time would be worth $300 an hour. I don't mean necessarily *charging* $300 an hour. I mean – *acting like it.*

This year, fueled by my newfound mental wealth, I've watched two things radically transform:

Who I decide to spend time with and how much of that time.

How I carry myself to make sure I'm delivering $300 an hour to myself and to others.

Nothing changed. Except my mindset.

And that changed *everything.*

Worth $300 an hour?

I'm not quite sure whether you're actually earning that *yet* or not is relevant.

Do you?

Why not try it on Monday? Just Monday.

Make every choice and carry out every action as if your time is worth $300 an hour.

Think about it this weekend:

What will you do?

What won't you do?

To whom will you say yes?

To whom will you say no?

Today's your lucky day. You just got a mental raise.

17. ARE YOU PRODUCTIVE OR JUST BUSY?

You start the day with the best of intentions. You have your to-do list in front of you, and you crank-start the first task and settle in.

A few moments go by and someone [drops by/calls/IMs/ swoops in on a bullwhip] to chitchat about work, play, reality TV, or other stuff.

They leave. You decide you better check your inbox. Nine new messages. Better run through those real quick, right?

Your to-do list weeps as your day ends and you just haven't gotten everything done, but you've been super busy.

Are you productive or just busy?

You get to choose, you know.

Close your day by defining the next day's most important tasks – the stuff that simply must get done tomorrow. Then prepare your workspace to begin immediately on the first of those tasks.

Then:

Get to work.

Start on task #1.

Do not check email.

Do not check voicemails.

Finish task #1.

You will feel the awesome.

Someone comes to your workspace and interrupts? Turn, and sincerely say:

"I'm so sorry. I'm really busy right now. Maybe you could shoot me an email, and I'll follow*-up later? Thank you."

Very important – at the asterisk – begin to turn your back to them and get back to your task. Close the feedback loop before they get a chance to continue the discussion.

Obviously, mileage varies by discretion. If it's your boss, you may not want to turn your back on her.

But you get to choose. You are not held hostage to your email, your voicemail, or cubicle lurkers.

Work as part of a department? Last thing of the day – share your most important tasks of the next day with each other and encourage and review with each other throughout the day.

Soon, you'll be shockingly productive and not simply busy all the time.

And, finally, if you're shocked, your co-workers are going to be doubly so. Let them know you're making some changes. Energy's infectious. Soon, they'll behave differently as well.

18. WHAT ARE PEOPLE PAYING YOU TO DO?

Let's talk for a moment about business model.

With shipping companies, we all understand that if we want something here tomorrow, we're going to pay a premium for it, right? If I'm not in as big a rush, I'll pay less. Until someone invents a different model, that's the baseline of our understanding of the shipping business. Customers are paying for speed.

What are people paying you to do? Are you leveraging that skill when it comes to your pricing?

Consider my business partner Rex's video production company, SunPop Studios. They produce extraordinarily authentic, unusual video snapshots of people and companies. They are very, very good at what they do. They charge accordingly.

For a set price, you fly to Austin (or Toronto or a growing list of locations) and you work with Rex and Jake and some others to do your video their way. Your finished product is extraordinary, and you get it quickly.

Unless you want to help.

If you want to offer your own creative input, that costs more.

That's right. If you want them to do exactly what you hired them to do (and do it as well as anyone in the world), it actually costs less than if you want to help them do it.

Have they probably lost some business as a result? Sure. Do you think they're infinitely happier with the clients they've pre-qualified through this "helper tax?" Sure.

It doesn't just take talent and insight, though, does it?

It takes guts.

Remember - there's a reason you sought them out.

Remember - there's a reason people are seeking you out. Charge accordingly.

19. REFUSING BUSINESS

"Guys, this is awkward and I don't quite know how to say this ... but you don't want to hire us today."

That's what I said to some incredibly kind and talented brothers and their father.

Wilhour Construction - makers of beautiful outbuildings and tool sheds in Illinois (soon to be in the Midwest).

I had come up to talk to them about advertising problems, and how we could possibly fix them.

They were ready to hire us. Money had already changed hands.

But after listening for close to forty-five minutes, it became clear their problems weren't advertising problems.

They were already growing too quickly on the merits of the quality of their work. The *last* thing they needed at this point was good advertising. They had staffing concerns and systems, and policies and procedures they needed to develop to grow their company to the next level.

Only then would they be ready for our services.

I left there that day losing a client, but gaining something more valuable: self-respect and the respect of others.

My father taught me that at an early age: *do the right thing it will come back to you tenfold.* It's the reason why - and I'm thankful that before I started my own company that my employers understood - that from the very beginning I haven't worked with strip clubs, adult bookstores or places of that nature.

I choose not to do those things. Sometimes the best thing we can do is tell someone "no."

It's good for the soul, don't you think?

My partner and mentor, Michele Miller, had some advice for me when I gave a talk to college students called *All The Difference.* It's about the lessons I've learned along this road less traveled.

Michele suggested they wake up each morning and wonder to what they'll say "no" to today. We say "yes" far too often. We commit to far too many things.

At what expense? To what will you say "no" today?

On what will you not compromise?

That day - at Wilhour - I said "no" to a large sum of money over the next year - or possibly five years - because it was the right thing to do.

When you realize a relationship is not meant to be, stop it as quickly as possible.

My business partner and worldwide poet and entertainer, Peter Nevland, shared his story with me just the other day about ... well, I'll let Peter tell you the story:

It's still fresh. We hung up the phone this morning, and a wave of relief washed over me. We had fired our first client. We've heard Roy and other partners talk about it, but some lessons can't be learned without doing.

We aren't knee-jerk, quick-to-blame kind of guys. We've endured eight months of working far too hard for a client who just didn't get it and fought our every piece of advice. What was worse, when he tried to implement our advice, he couldn't. He had a poor programmer whose favorite phrase was, "That just can't be done with X-Cart," and a graphic designer who was his nineteen-year old son. We probably should have seen this in the beginning. At least we're free now.

Two things happened when we first brought up the idea of parting ways:

1.   He began to take our advice seriously.

We couldn't believe that he started agreeing with us about things that he had vehemently disagreed with only days prior. He also took a serious look at how poorly his team executed. He is now focused on fixing his team and implementing our advice. We'll see if he comes through.

2.   We began to feel hopeful about life again.

We've worked way too hard hoping that their team would finally "get it." Every positive sign only delivered fresh failure, new disappointments. "How could people be so stupid?" we thought. It's amazing how much more time I now have to do things like breathe, write, take care of other clients and pursue more business. Yes, I miss the money, but I have great confidence that more will come my way.

We chose a gracious firing that took a couple conversations, but let him know that we cared about him and his business. He remains open to us working together in the future, and we remain skeptical. He also values what we've given him and would gladly recommend us to other businesses. That may not be your style. But we've found that it's the best one for both us.

You can read more about Peter and listen to his amazing words at www.spokengroove.com.

20. THE SEVEN FACETS OF PROFESSIONALISM

1. Appearance

Whether it's never seeing trash at Disney or your heating and air conditioning technician slipping floor savers over his shoes, we notice the look, sound and smell of the persons, places and things with which we do business.

Even if the coffee house hipster barista sports her skinny jeans and Residents t-shirt, we still expect a certain degree of cleanliness and order to her rumples. The same holds true for your parking lot, your service vans and your bathroom.

2. Attentiveness

Look me in the eye. Acknowledge you've seen me and are preparing to engage with me. When it's my turn, don't excuse me for the person calling on the phone.

In his book *Entreleadership*, Dave Ramsey tells the story of the pizza delivery driver who watched his tips increase when he began jogging from his car to the door. Make us feel like we matter. It's really not that hard. We have to do business with each other anyway, so the quicker you can help me, the quicker I'll be out of your life.

3. Dependability

Can we count on you to do what you say you're going to do when you say you're going to do it? Typically, an absence of dependability becomes shareworthy.

4. Consistency

I wrote about consistency in the same post last week. Consistency is the dependability of your dependability. You need systems, policies, and procedures to deliver dependability, umm, dependably.

5. Focus

A customer at hand isn't just an important thing – it's the only thing that matters at any given moment. The best servers in restaurants have this down, don't they? She might have fifteen tables, but you'd never know it.

Restaurant owner Laura Harbaugh called it "The Three Second Rule."

I may only be speaking with you for three seconds, but for those three seconds I'm locked in. You are the only thing that matters to me in the world.

It's harder than ever amidst the growing distractions. It's also more important than ever. [Read more about Laura's awesomeness in Chapter 36.]

6. Proactivity

I originally had nine facets of each main component, but I realized that a couple were really pretty much the same. I originally had both *proactivity* and *authority*.

What I mean is – for example – that any Ritz Carlton employee can comp up to $100 worth of services to make something right on the spot. The best business owners train their employees, then give them the authority to make decisions the owner will support even when they don't necessarily agree with it.

Read Carl Sewell's *Customers For Life* if you want to learn more about this.

7. Simplification

Technological, ahem, advances have helped companies build walls in the name of "customer convenience."

Please. Did any customer ever ask for an automated phone tree? The layers of complexity in today's work and world increase friction. We're faster, busier, multi-tasking, aggressive, noisy creatures that demand attention NOW.

Shareworthy Service providers have a gift of being able to evaluate a complex situation and quickly distill it down and remove any tension or friction. You can just feel tense situations deflate at Apple's Genius Bars when a twenty-two-year-old uses common language to describe an otherwise technical problem to a seventy-five-year-old laptop owner. Watch a great guest services manager in Las Vegas hear a problem, understand a problem, and fix a problem quickly and quietly.

There you go. Those are the first heavy seven.

How does your company rate with each? Do you actually have systems and policies in place to point these facets in your favor, or are y'all just winging it?

21. THE PERFECT CLIENT MEETING

You know how many perfect meetings I've had in my life? One. But I liked it so much that I pulled over in a gas station on the way home and deconstructed it.

Be between five and ten minutes early. Have your materials ready.

Greet warmly. Ask something specific about family. Memory matters.

Ask how they're tracking.

Go over agenda.

Work the agenda. Review obligations.

Answer questions as asked.

Listen quietly and completely. Make eye contact.

Have an opinion. Be honest.

Get clarity on deliverables, assignments, and deadlines. If next meeting needs to be set, set it now!

Say goodbye. Get back to work.

That's it. If you don't have all those elements, meetings need to be improved.

22. HOW TO IMPROVE YOUR NEXT BRAINSTORMING SESSION

Having sat through a few thousand brainstorming sessions over the years I feel I'm reasonably qualified when I say with all certainty that most brainstorming sessions are wildly flawed.

If you'd like to get infinitely more out of your company's next brainstorming session, here are a few tips for you:

Number one, make sure people know the goals and what it is you'll be trying to make happen. Do this in advance. Say you have a brainstorming lunch at your company every Friday - then by no later than Thursday morning, you should email out what you are trying to accomplish to everyone who's going to participate. In fact, send them to everyone in the organization - even those who can't attend.

As I learned from Dr. Richard D. Grant about personality types - approximately half of your organization are introverts who draw energy from processing ideas internally and alone. This doesn't mean they're necessarily shy, but it does mean they consider ideas and concepts in their own mind and are usually only willing to share after having giving a particular problem some thought.

The other half, extraverts, will gladly come to a brainstorming session and share anything that's on their mind at any time. They probably didn't read the email you sent.

Because of this difference between the two personality types, typical brainstorming sessions are usually dominated by these extraverts ... because an introvert would rather have their toenails pulled out one by one than speak when they haven't first had a chance to process the information.

Introverts don't like to speak off the top of their heads. They like to think about things first.

By sending the agenda of the problems you're trying to solve in advance, you will give the introverts time to think about these things.

During your session, keep things moving. It should be someone's job - maybe not yours, but someone's - to make sure that all the topics get addressed and that things keep flowing. A timer is critical. Don't attempt necessarily to contribute yourself. Keep notes. Consider recording the sessions. If you have five topics in an hour, each gets about ten minutes.

After the session and by day's end, you are responsible for sending a recap of what was discussed along with the following challenge: "Please take the next couple days and think if you have any other ideas or solutions - no matter how strange or silly - that might possibly help with the problems we were trying to solve today. Here's a list of them. By noon on Monday (or whatever), please leave me a voicemail or send me an email with your thoughts. Thanks everyone!"

This will not only give extraverts and introverts alike, focus and clarity on the problems you're trying to solve, but it will give the introverts the benefit of time to process their thoughts and ideas, and it will at least double the productivity of your next brainstorming session.

Emails. Follow through. Goals. Clarity. Thanks, Dr. Grant.

23. BIG X. LITTLE X.

Sometimes it's as simple as asking someone:

"What is it you're trying to make happen?"

Then asking:

"Okay. What's holding you back?"

Oftentimes they know. Or at least they know symptoms, if not the actual root cause.

I often use a treasure map metaphor. Draw out an island. Put a little 'x' and a big 'X' on there. The little 'x' is where they are today. The big 'X' is where they want to be.

Start by asking them to describe what the big 'X' looks and feels like.

Then ask them to describe the little 'x' - where they are today.

Then draw a dotted line between the two and ask them how long it's going to take us to get from one to the other.

Once they answer that question, ask them: "What obstacles do you *know* we're going to face?"

Listen.

Then, after everything, ask them simply ... "Okay ... what's the first step?"

24. RECORDING CONVERSATIONS

Speaking of recording conversations, one of the most important things I've learned, I learned in 1997 from Christine Coyle - a fellow Saluki and one of the great copywriting minds of the 20th century.

Christine taught me to record conversations with clients. This is so important on so many levels, and you're right - at first, they will be apprehensive.

Here's what I tell them:

I say, "I'm going to be at your place next Tuesday for our first conversation, and I know this might seem a little strange, and I'm happy to sign any nondisclosure agreement you would like me to sign, but I would like to record our conversation, and I'll tell you why.

"One, I hate having my head buried in the notebook while we're talking. I know there will be things are really, really, really important and might take us down really, really, really interesting, helpful, important rabbit holes, but we may miss all that because I'm trying to write stuff down.

"This way, I don't have to remember what you said. It's all there for me later when I start the critical phase of building our strategy. You'll see me jot down time signatures, so I know to reference it later. I have ten-year-old conversations in the archive that I still reference. I'm hoping this is the beginning of something equally special and important.

"Remember, I'm a vault. I'm willing to be held legally accountable for being a vault."

That's what I tell clients, and it's all true.

But what else is important is this: if you can make eye contact and have confidence in your client to open up, and he or she sees that you're engaged in the conversation and you're leaning forward and listening and nodding, that's a signal to your client that what they're saying matters.

Do you get that? It might sound self-evident, but I can assure you that after watching hundreds of sales representatives disconnect, it needs stating.

The client doesn't get that sense of connecting when your head is buried in a notebook.

If you can listen ... really listen ... it gives you credibility, and your client confidence to open up. It shows them that you are not the same person who's come in a million times and asked him the same twenty-seven questions they've been asked a million times.

If you ask stupid, shallow questions, don't be surprised when you get stupid, shallow answers.

By setting aside the notebook, by recording the conversation, by signaling that you're willing to be sued if you betray them, you will get far more out of your interview subject.

Look them in the eye. Stay engaged. Actively listen. Follow along.

Support them. Remember, you're both in this together.

25. CRITICAL THINKING

Have you worked on your critical thinking? Do you practice it?

It helps.

And criticism doesn't simply mean saying something "sucks." It means understanding why something doesn't or does work. (Living in a college town with a renowned J-School, I've witnessed countless experts-before-their-times denounce things without reason.)

Let me clarify:

• Buy another little notebook.

• Read a short story, listen to a radio advertisement, watch a television show, peruse a website.

• In your little notebook, articulate WHY you feel it works or it doesn't.

Understand? You need not share or publish these critical opinions, but you need to have them.

You'll think it'll be easy, but I betcha you'll discover it's surprisingly difficult at first to articulate your thoughts. But as you progress, you'll find yourself ever gaining confidence in meetings with your clients. Even better? You'll amass a nice canon of your own critical thoughts, and statements of your own writing principles.

Don't worry others may disagree with you. It's not about sharing these moments with others - it's merely practice to improve your ability to parse what works, what doesn't, and why.

Just bleating out loud that something "sucks" quickly makes you a bore. Why does it suck? Why was it awesome? Answering those questions well will prove harder than you might suspect.

Quietly practice having a critical opinion.

Don't stop at suck.

26. NOTEBOOK MOMENTS

Tim - May the strong drink allow us to writer closer, rather than create a bunch of bumbling fools. We Must Proceed On.
~ Joshua Stevens

Spoils of future success?

My first strategist tool-kit upgrade came courtesy of Josh.

For years, I'd carried around the ubiquitous $0.39 top-spiral notebook. I wore a wallet/chew-faded pattern into the back left-pocket of several pairs of blue jeans. As a professional observer paid to capture and re-interpret the human condition, it seemed silly to me not to write down the stolen little moments between those strange and wonderful to me.

Curiosity - that theme keeps popping up, eh?

And it's curiosity that has led me to note little interactions between people. Not big stories, but small phrases or interesting micro-vignettes that clicked with me.

"Click."

Dick Orkin and Christine Coyle taught me to recognize "click" moments like a photographer snapping the shutter. Capturing a moment in time, only within my frame (and outside it for that matter) are words, not visual images.

But remember, verbal suggestions can create mental images.

The goal with your notebook - whether the $0.39 variety or the fancy ten dollar Moleskine version gifted and inscribed to me by Josh - should be to simply capture any such moment that clicks.

Don't judge or analyze the moments. Leave the left brain out of this. Just document them.

For it's these little notebook moments that will provide context for your stories, and they'll resonate with others.

Prepare to watch your ads leap off the page, reach out their hands, and hold a mirror up to reality.

I think I'll elaborate more before moving on. In the next chapter, we'll visit the Notebook Moment Hall of Fame. Then we'll look at a recent example of four young ladies and their Oprah.

27. ZEN & THE ART OF NOTEBOOK MOMENTS

<<< [Int: Monk's Diner w / Jerry and Jean-Paul]

Jerry: (pause) *So what happened? The snooze alarm, wasn't it?*

Jean-Paul: *Man, it wasn't the snooze. Most people think it was the snooze, but no, no snooze.*

Jerry: *AM/PM.*

Jean-Paul: *Man, it wasn't the AM/PM. It was the volume.*

Jerry: *Ahhh, the volume.*

Jean-Paul: *Yes, the volume. There was a separate knob for the radio alarm.*

Jerry: *Ahhh, separate knob.*

Jean-Paul: *Yes, separate knob. Why separate knob?!? Why separate knob?!?* (frustrated)

Jerry: *Some people like to have the radio alarm a little louder than the radio.*

Jean-Paul: *Oh, please, man, please!*

(From *Seinfeld* "The Hot Tub" - Originally broadcast 10/19/95; written by Gregg Kavet & Andy Robin)

Notice how they never say hotel or alarm clock.

In the last chapter, I urged you to purchase a small notebook and collect little moments of nothing - those little phrases/conversations you pick up while eavesdropping on the world that "click" a shutter in your mental camera.

Or, if you can't make it out tonight, simply flip through your television channels until you come across someone showing *Seinfeld* in syndication.

They got it. Heck, they celebrated it. They flaunted in our faces the fact that their show was about nothing. So are our lives. We connect to one another through a series of little interconnected moments that make us say "Yep! I've been there."

So many businesses want to fill their advertising with grand statements and sweeping stuffs. Problem is we don't live our lives in grand statements.

We relate to the little moments. We live in the interstitials. We connect to nothings. Those, then, should be your focus.

We connect dots.

Waiting for my airplane to push back from the terminal, I listened to four late-twenty-something young ladies passionately arguing the merits of treadmills or black pumps or something when one of the young ladies - in a lather - bolstered her argument by prefacing it with:

"Well ... Oprah says ..."

I am suspect of any argument that begins, "Well ... Oprah says," and I was willing to bet more than a few other men were, too.

Thus, one of my clients - a sports bar - began the first ever men's night whose launch ad closed with just that line. It was a huge success with much rejoicing.

28. 21 KILLER RECRUITMENT QUESTIONS

Years ago, before I had some success helping my clients write "those weird kinds" of recruitment ads, Roy confirmed what I intuitively suspected: the best ads aren't about the position, but about the person you hope to hire.

Write your ads about your ideal person.

To be specific, you'll need to ask yourself (and others) some questions to better define that person before you can hope to find them.

And before you can ever expect to ask great questions to the right person across the table from you in an interview, you're going to have to ask yourself (and your current employees) some questions to help you build the right recruitment message.

Here are fourteen questions you can ask yourself – followed by seven more you should consider asking people in your company – specifically, if possible, those who currently occupy the same position.

Yes, some of them require some speculation. Use your imagination. You get to build your dream person, remember.

Fourteen Questions To Ask Yourself

1.   Describe to me what an ideal day in the life of this job would be.

2. Tell me about the ideal candidate's temperament. Why is that important?

3. What's in it for her if she says yes? Why should she leave what she's doing now?

4. Are you giving this person more free time or more money than she has now?

5. Are you giving this person more opportunity or more security than she has now?

6. What would impress you about the right candidate in an interview? A question she would ask? Some research she would have done?

7. Does this person need any special skills?

8. What sort of values does this person hold dear?

9. What do you suspect your ideal person likes to do in her leisure time?

10. If you were going to hire from within – who among your current staff is your best model for this position ... why?

11. The person you hire exceeds beyond your wildest dreams ... really successful in all the right ways ... it's a year from today and everything is rocking for the office due in no small part to what your new hire has done ... what has she done? Be specific. Paint that picture of success for me.

12. Realistically, what could the right person doing extremely well earn in the first year ... and don't give me that salary commensurate with experience b.s., or "your potential is unlimited b.s. ... there is a limit ... what is it?

13. What will be the most frustrating thing about the job?

14. What is your call to action? What would you like this person to do as a result of being persuaded by the ad?

Seven Questions for Current Employees of Your Company:

1. What did you do before you starting working here?
2. What's the best thing about your job?
3. What's the worst thing?
4. What's a typical day like?
5. What's the worst day like?
6. What other occupations might be good at this?
7. If you had any advice for someone starting out in this job, what might it be?

Explain to them that their answers are between us ... we just want to get a better feel for how to hire someone just like them since their bosses spoke highly of them.

Be prepared.

By doing this sort of prep work, you're going to get less applicants. I hope you won't miss sorting through dozens, if not hundreds, of unqualified applicants.

What you'll see immediately – by having specific answers to these questions – is a smaller number of more qualified prospects for your open positions.

Sheesh! Isn't this more work for us??

Absolutely.

29. ARE Y'ALL ON THE SAME PAGE?

Wanna do something scary? Ask each employee the following questions, BUT ... don't let them compare answers. You want each person to answer independently because you want to see where their answers converge and diverge with yours and with each other's.

What is it we're trying to make happen?

What's a happy ending? When we throw a HUGE blowout party to celebrate, what just happened?

Why are we there now? What's holding us back?

Back to number one - break it down? What are our goals, then, to get to the party?

Now, prioritize them. Which one do we need to tackle first? Second? Third?

If money were no object, how would we solve the first problem?

Okay, so money is an object, so what's the first step to solving the first problem?

Do you know what your employees believe? Does it bother you that you don't know?

Now, you want to take it a step further? Ask your customers.

30. FOLLOWING UP

Wait. That's not it. Your employees, and hopefully your customers (you daring rascal, you), made the effort to give you their honest thoughts and opinions.

Now, you have to do the heavy lifting. You have to gather the data yourself, evaluate it, and follow up with each person with gratitude. Is this a lot of work?

Absolutely.

Then ... you have to measure and reward the best of these initiatives. You need to recognize the effort, and you need to reward successful execution of those efforts.

Are you willing to swing that hammer? You better be in this day and age, yo.

31. "NEVER TOO HIGH ...
NEVER TOO LOW ..."

Were you aware there's a management theory that states you need to be very careful not to praise your employees too much?

That's right – don't give your employees too much praise. Don't spend too much time pointing out the things they do well. It might give them big heads or cause them to start coasting or give them scurvy or something.

Evidently, you shouldn't be overly critical nor should you be overly complimentary.

The catchphrase on the Lumberghian coffee mug would read:

"Never too high ... Never too low ..."

I've been thinking about this theory for close to awhile now, and I've come to the following conclusion:

If that's not the stupidest thing I've ever heard, it's at least in the conversation.

After I thought about this and wrote it what you just read, I shared it with my friend Jeff Sexton. He's much smarter than me. This is not hyperbole. Ask anyone who knows us both.

He said:

Tim,

I used to work for a consulting firm that helped hospitals raise their patient satisfaction scores. So you might think the first thing we worked on with clients was how to make their patients happier. But you'd be wrong. The first thing we worked on was how to make the nurses happier. Happy employees = Happy customers. The founder of our company got that from Southwest Airlines.

Do you think it's a coincidence that all these very successful companies have the same concept of employee satisfaction?

I don't...

- Jeff

Way to go, Mr. Happypants.

32. EAT THE HAGGIS

If you don't know what it is, go look up "haggis."

I know, right??

I ate it.

On a once in a lifetime trip to Scotland, a place I've only been dreaming of visiting since I was twelve, I ate the haggis.

And it tasted about like you expected it might.

But that's kind of irrelevant, isn't it?

For years, I would find reasons to avoid stepping out onto the skinny end of the branch.

Now I look back and think, "How sad."

Quiet desperation's for suckers.

Plug in.

Say yes.

Climb out onto the skinny end.

Pass the haggis.

TIM MILES

KEEPING

TIM MILES

33. WHY CALL IT SHAREWORTHY?

To: Michele Miller, Lynn Peisker, Ryan Patrick, Scott Cox, Dee Miles, Jane Fraser, Scott Fraser, Sarah Ripley, Craig Arthur, Adam Donmoyer, Jeff Sexton, Rhiannon Trask, Laura Harris, Paul Boomer, Heidi Crouch, Roy H. Williams, Jeffrey Eisenberg, Tom Wanek:

Hi there. I'm finishing up a new presentation on, essentially, The Ten Commandments of Legendary Customer Service. But I want a different word than "legendary."

World-class?

Special?

Remarkable?

Gobsmacking? (Would love, I think, to go with a Seussian word that's mine alone but totally works ... much like the 'waka waka' diamond ...)

Bigtastic?

Any thoughts? I'd be grateful. Thanks!

t

I wanted something that said - good or bad - "I want to tell others about this experience."

But I wanted something else, too.

I wanted something that said to a company, "We're all in this together."

71

I had inadvertently written it in another email when I said:

What would make something shareworthy?

At a lunch two days later, my friend Rhiannon said, "Here it is. Right here in your email."

Chicks are smarter than guys, yo.

And so, Shareworthy Customer Service was born.

Can your company:

Develop a plan to implement policies and procedures that arouse such delight in customers that they head to Facebook and Twitter and their blogs to brag about you?

Create a sustainable program that clearly and authentically points everyone - from CEO to part-time employees - toward the same North Star?

How can you make your customer service shareworthy?

34. SMILE! YOU JUST OPENED A SMALL BUSINESS.

"You just opened a small business."

Years ago, a good friend and client at the time (a dentist), explained to me why so many *technicians* struggle when they open their practices.

In dental school, students studied amalgams and x-rays and maybe even how to use that cool little suction thingie.

So, a technician graduates well-schooled in the arts of her science – whether that science is dentistry, medicine, photography or whatever.

But my friend said to me, "That same person doesn't have any real understanding of how to run a business."

I bring this up for two reasons:

1. *Dilbert* creator Scott Adams wrote a fantastic essay for the Journal about education and entrepreneurship – what he thinks should be taught vs. what is actually taught viewed through the lens of his actual college experience. Read it. I'd love to hear what you think.

2. Our friend Rhiannon.

Rhiannon recently left behind an impressive professional résumé as VP of Marketing for a regional bank to pursue her dream of being a professional photographer.

She's a tremendous photographer. But, really, isn't that the easy part?

Not for you or me, I mean, but for anyone who would even remotely consider accepting money to take pictures.

You know what I mean ... that's kind of the basic prerequisite for this sorta thing, right?

What impressed us – or, more correctly, my wife – after we used her for a recent family photo session was her firm grasp on the fact that she "just opened a small business."

Rhiannon, and her company Lollipop Photography:

Sent a thoroughly detailed email to Mama (who booked the appointment) a couple days before the shoot outlining exactly what we could expect.

Knew who was boss from the moment we arrived: Mama. If she could keep Mama happy, she knew everyone would be happy.

Understood that to keep Mama happy, she had to be totally flexible with the whims and fancies of two young children – one of whom has special needs. In other words, every time Will started making silly faces or Sarah started running to another tree, Rhiannon acted as though that was EXACTLY what she had in mind for the next shot. She was brilliantly flexible but always prepared to shoot.

Delivered a longer, better experience than promised.

Transferred delight and confidence throughout the shoot - which continually kept Mama at ease – this, in spite of the fact, that we were at times ready to place our daughter on eBay.

Conveyed clear expectations of when we could expect to see photos – which is really what matters more than anything. How quickly can you have those shots online so Mama can see them and share them with her friends.

Not just beat … but reeeeeally beat that expectation by more than forty-eight hours. The last time we used a portrait photography studio, they were great photographers who worked well with our son. They were kind, patient and fun. Then it was our turn to be patient as it took more than three weeks to get those photos up and online. Mama was displeased. Do not displease Mama.

Plus, we get the digital files on CD. Why? Because that's the way we wanted them, and that's the way more and more families want to receive their pictures. So many photographers still think it's 1973, and force us to buy expensive printed portraits. No thank you.

That evening, as we were checking out our photos through the wonderful AppleTV, two of Dee's mama mafia – Heidi and Heather – came over and ooooh'd and aaaaah'd.

Money's worth. She could have charged twice the price, but in fact, as our friends swore they'd use Rhiannon next time, she – in fact – tripled her money's worth, and possibly more – as those pictures spread like mama-fueled wildfire through social media.

Rhiannon's starting off successfully not because she's a great photographer, though she is, but because Rhiannon understands what too few do — that she just opened a small business — and it's why I think she's the best Columbia photographer working today.

35. SIMPLIFYING SHAREWORTHY

The Reverend Harold T. Mooney taught me to love God and golf. He was able to simplify both for me.

When we'd talk about golf at the driving range or in the big emerald yard behind the church, he'd say, "Tim – so many people want to confuse the issue with movements and swing thoughts and where the left wrist should be at impact.

"It gets your brain so full, it's impossible to perform.

"Simplify the game down to what matters," he said. "Two things – study two things, think about two things, practice two things, and you'll learn to master the game.

"Golf," Fr. Mooney said, "comes down to direction and distance. Nothing more or less."

ALS – Lou Gehrig's Disease – took one of my heroes much too quickly, but I remember the lesson, Father.

After researching hundreds of stories, reading a half-dozen books and interviewing a few world-class company leaders, I've realized – as I'm sure you have as well – that recognizing delightful and spectacular customer service isn't really all that hard.

In fact, the same fourteen characteristics that seem to define magnificent and remarkable customer service pop up time and again in story after story.

But so did something else. Another pattern emerged after a couple hundred hours of research these past couple months – something even simpler.

While there are fourteen manifestations, fourteen defining characteristics, fourteen ways to deliver delight, those fourteen fall evenly into two halves.

Study these two things.

Think about these two things.

Practice these two things, and you'll learn to master the game.

After researching hundreds of stories, two common threads tie them all together:

1.   Professionalism
2.   Kindness

Each has seven links that shoot off to deliver these characteristics to the customer, but if you wish to boil it down to the basic building blocks of all shareworthy customer service stories, it's those two, bub: Professionalism and Kindness.

I told you it was simple. Just like golf, it's simple to read about or watch – the greats make it looks so effortless, don't they? The Apples and the Disneys and the Zapposeseses.

Heck, it's even relatively easy to start to play the game yourself, isn't it?

But mastery ... going pro? Well ... it's, frankly, just as simple.

It's just not easy.

36. LAURA HARBAUGH'S MAGIC NUMBER

A wise man once said, "Three is the number, and the number shall be three."

That wise man would have liked Laura Harbaugh.

Harbaugh was one of the first people who piqued my interest when I moved to Carbondale, Illinois to attend Southern Illinois University.

She was a waitress at Quatro's Pizza who always made remarkable eye contact, who always seemed - what's the word – *genuine,* and never seemed to be in a rush or stressed out - which is atypical for young servers in busy restaurants.

Laura went on to achieve the American dream.

In the late '90s, she opened a restaurant of her own, and Harbaugh's café was born - not far from Quatro's pizza.

She has many secrets I'm sure, but there are three things that have always impressed me about her and the way she runs her business.

The first of which is that she seems to understand what matters and what doesn't. She focuses on what matters. That's easier said than done, isn't it? I find it interesting that her coffee cups are a collection of donations, thrift shop pickups, and apparently whatever she had lying around her house when she opened the restaurant.

I think it's perfect. It communicates a language about the feeling of the restaurant. So often business owners leave things to chance and don't consciously make decisions about lighting, staffing, decor, or parking spaces. These, too, are part of any business's brand.

The second thing Laura does that impresses me so deeply - and she must have learned this from watching so many servers over the years - is that if you want to work at Harbaugh's, fine. You're going to audition.

You want to wait tables? Audition.

Show us that you're capable of handling a shift. There's no more evidence we'll need that you'll work here. Okay, sure, you have to fill out an application, and we have to check your references, but the best reference of all is you demonstrating your ability in the context of a working day.

I think that it's probably the third of the three that impresses me most and is the best lesson for anyone reading this.

Laura may not even remember telling me this, but it's something I've used for more than a dozen years. She told me once when I was working on a project for her television ad, that her secret - a secret she passes on to her staff - is that when you're talking with the customer you must give them your full undivided attention.

This is easier than it sounds in the course of a busy day with many tables and other customers to remember.

Laura said to me - and I remember it like it was yesterday and not the summer of 2001 - "Even if it's only three seconds with a customer, for those three seconds that customer is the most important thing to me in the world."

In this day and age of smartphones and Twitter and text messaging, where we're all a little twitchy to see what else is going on - that might be the most important lesson of all:

Give something or someone the gift of your full, undivided attention.

37. THE FOURTEEN FACETS OF SHAREWORTHY SERVICE

Over the past couple months, I've spent countless hours researching studies and stories of customer service. I've read the horror stories, and I've heard the stories of spectacular, shareworthy service.

I'm sure you have your own stories in both corners.

As I did my research, patterns emerged.

Think of the foundation of shareworthy service as two big honkin' rocks – each with seven facets.

Every shareworthy story is built from this list. I originally started with eighteen facets, but I realized that a few were so closely related that I simplified things.

I'm going to share stories with you of world-beating customer service and delight. In these, you'll see these fourteen facets recur time and again. I'll point them out to you. It's pretty neat, actually – out of hundreds of stories, I couldn't find anything that didn't fit the pattern.

Then I'll show you how to leverage these facets into your company's own unique system for defining, measuring and rewarding shareworthy service.

Big Honkin' Rock #1: Professionalism

1. Appearance
2. Attentiveness
3. Consistency
4. Dependability

5. Focus
6. Pro-activity
7. Simplification

Big Honkin' Rock #2: Kindness

1. Active Listening
2. Empathy
3. Engagement
4. Memory
5. Manners
6. Playfulness
7. Privilege

There you go. Those are the heavy seven-plus-seven.

And they apply whether you live in Columbus, Caracas, or Carbondale.

Think of your own stories of shareworthy service. Can you think of anything remarkable that wasn't reflected in one of the fourteen facets above?

38. BETH'S BEST CUSTOMERS

I've had a lot of success helping home services companies: roofing, water treatment, heating & air conditioning.

No, it's not terribly exciting, on the surface, at least.

As my first HVAC client said in our first meeting: "Air conditioning isn't sexy."

Nope, so how did I learn to help grow these companies by double digits?

It was easy, actually. I was dumb, so I listened. A lot.

And that first home services company - Chapman Heating & Cooling - gave me a very important lesson about how to run a business in that same meeting.

Beth Chapman, sweet and brilliant, told me about - as the owner - her most important customers.

"My most important customers are our employees. If they're not happy, if they're not given everything they need to succeed, then how can we expect them to treat our paying customers well?

"For our customers to win, our employees have to win first."

She really saw it that simply, and it was clear it wasn't just lip service around they shop. The Chapman family made it their number one, two and three priority: to make sure their customers - the Chapman employees - were delighted.

Another friend, Matt, CFO at The River - a fiercely independent Contemporary Christian radio station in Columbus, Ohio, put it another way:

"The leader's role is simply to create an environment where his or her employees can do their best work, evaluate that work, and reward the results of that work."

That's it. Don't complicate it.

Do you view your company that way?

You can simplify it still if you're a larger organization. As a C-level executive, can you regard your ONLY customers as your managers and department heads? That's it. If you focused on no one else for a week, what might happen?

If you built systems, policies, procedures and methods for measurement and rewarding that process, what might happen to your organization?

Would it give you more time? Would it give you more focus? What's the worst thing that would happen if you gave all your energy and passion to a small number of your best customers and empowered and rewarded them for doing the same?

Why don't you give it a try? I don't mean form a committee. I mean: *Do. It.* What's the first step in trying it?

Okay. There. You're out of reasons not to do it.

Thanks, Beth. Thanks, Matt.

39. THE SEVEN FACETS OF KINDNESS

Shareworthy service – either good or bad – has two main components: Professionalism and Kindness. Each component has seven facets.

In Chapter 20, I examined the seven facets of Professionalism – the boring bedrocks of any successful company. Now, we get to talk about Professionalism's fun baby sister: Kindness.

Kindness gets all the headlines and wins all the awards. Kindness is splashy and silly, and three-exclamation-point-all-caps FUN!!!

1. Active Listening

You can usually tell when people are dialed in, can't you? Active listening changes your expression. Your head leans forward, and you fidget less – if at all. You're really hearing someone's problem, challenge, or situation. It builds confidence in the person telling the story.

You can dazzle them by repeating back the essence of what they said "just to make sure you have it right." So many people today don't listen actively. They seem merely to be waiting for the other person to finish so they can start talking again. Sound familiar? The good news is you can practice your active listening skills.

2. Empathy

I actually don't believe the customer is always right, do you? Sometimes, the customer is uniquely unqualified to assess what's best for them. That said, an expert at empathy understands the delicate bridge connecting what the customer wants and what the customer needs.

Put yourself in the customer's shoes, then use the benefit of your expertise to simply show them what they'd really prefer to do if they had your knowledge and skill set.

3. Engagement

Engaged people give off a contagious energy. Your company's next superstar, in fact, is out there right now willing to dazzle you with his or her eyes and smile and personality. You may just have to pull up to the second window to find her.

A former colleague taught me this a long time ago: Keep some cards with you. If you get engaging service at a drive-through, for example, hand the engager a card and suggest they come in for an interview for a sales position with your company.

Think about it – if someone can greet you with bright eyes and a smile at the drive through window of Long John Silver's – imagine what she could do making eight to ten times that much without her clothes having to, umm, smell like that every day. You know engaged people when you see them. You know the bright eyes and the locked-in, nothing-else-matters-but-you look.

4. Memory

For reasons passing understanding, I can still remember the birthdays of everyone in my eighth grade class (Steve – Oct. 5).

The good news is that this carried over into adulthood. I make a point – an effort – to remember the names of people's children and what they've been working on lately.

I remember a person's favorite drink or what kind of foods they don't like.

If you struggle with these things, why not use something like Evernote or some other syncable application to make notes of them. That's how your stylist does it, you know.

5. Manners

My father, a Marine, and my mother, raised in a family surrounded by schoolteachers, taught us "yes, sir" and "yes ma'am" values at a very early age. I would rather you tell me my children are polite and respectful than that they're smart or talented or good looking. There's simply no substitute for respect.

6. Playfulness

Lord, give us both the ability to take things seriously and the ability to be silly and fun. And please, Lord, give us the wisdom to know when each is appropriate. I ask you, though, wouldn't it be far more remarkable for a place to loosen up and have a little fun more often?

Wouldn't most interactions with most businesses be improved with a little fun? Like when I got that colonoscopy a couple months ago. I tell ya, the doctor had me in stitches. He said the funniest thing as he was getting ready to ... wait, maybe this is a story better saved for another day.

7. Privilege

I wrote about privilege last week. We like to be made to feel special. We like perks and treats and the perception that we're getting some degree of preferential treatment – even if it's policy. For example, we stayed at the Vdara Hotel in Vegas when I spoke at a company's annual meeting a few months back. I'd call down, and the guy would say:

"Hello, Mr. Miles. This is Stephen. How can I help you this evening?"

Look, I know my name pops up on a screen. I don't care. I feel like Elvis or Prince or somebody. I know the next guy who calls – his name is popping up on the same screen. I don't care. I fall for it every time. It's the little things.

Vegas is a fine hub for shareworthy service. So are many resorts in the Caribbean. I think we'd all do well to do some research in one or both of those places, don't you?

40. HOW TO IMPLEMENT SHAREWORTHY SERVICE

You cannot improve what you do not measure and reward.

Hold a company meeting.

Pass around pieces of paper. Tell them to put their names at the top.

Say:

We're not going to share answers with each other; in fact, I'm not going to ask you to write down answers, but I want you to write down questions.

Throughout the next twenty-five minutes or so, I'm going to give you a list of questions.

I want you to write them down.

Take the questions home and talk about them with your spouse or your significant other.

One week from today, I want you to turn in your answers.

Then, ask them these questions:

Number one: What's your dream vacation? You don't have to write the answer right now, just write down the question. Think about it.

Number two: If you had an extra week off from work, if you had an extra week's vacation, what would you do on that week off?

Number three: What big girl or big boy toy would you like the most right now? What absolutely selfish purchase would you like to make for yourself right now? And again, you're just writing down the questions.

Number four: If you could sort of turn the mirror around and help somebody else, what is your dream service project? Write that down. And what I mean by that is, is there something at your church? Some charity that you support? If the whole company got behind it, what would it be? So what's your dream service project is a short way to write that.

Number five: What's your dream meal? If we were going to take you out to dinner, what's your dream meal?

The last question for now is number six: If you were going to get a gift for your spouse or your significant other, what would that gift be?

As you continue to grow your company, the marketing budget will continue to increase. The marketing budget will continue to increase as a percentage of sales.

But there's a different between marketing and advertising.

Marketing continues to work as well as it ever has. The internet tends to make good marketing work more quickly.

Advertising - throwing stuff onto a T.V. or a radio, putting stuff in mailboxes - is working less and less well by the second for unremarkable companies.

Marketing is every touch point you have with a customer and no one touches them directly more than the employees in your little meeting - the ones answering questions about the things *they want and about which they dream.* No one.

And the internet's changed everything.

Ask in your meeting:

Now, can anyone tell me a story about terrible customer service?

Let the discussion simmer and marinade.

Then ask:

Now, with a show of hands, can you remember recently reading about one of your friends having or sharing a bad customer experience with a business on Facebook or Twitter or somewhere social?

Just go on Facebook any given day and you'll see somebody who was ticked off about something.

Advertising will put that business out of business faster.

Advertising only accelerates what's going to happen anyway. A great advertising campaign that draws more people to a bad business just spreads the word faster that this business stinks.

Then ask:

Now, what about legendary, spectacular customer service? Who's got a story?

It doesn't seem we have as many of those stories, does it?

There are the usual companies - the Apple Computer, the Zapposes. Nordstrom is another one.

The companies that make people want to talk about shareworthy stuff.

People get on Facebook and actually say great things.

Those companies? Advertising accelerates their growth logarithmically.

Boom! It takes off because they're making more people aware, and reminding people who've done business with the company, how awesome it was.

Have you ever been to Disney?

They literally wrote the book, a binder; you can't buy it. It's tall-stack-of-pancakes-thick with systems, policies and procedures on how to be awesome. How to make everyone feel like it's the best experience they ever had.

Here's what's funny: everybody who works at Disney works eight hours just like you and me, you know what I'm saying?

It requires no extra effort, or time, or money to be awesome than it does to be crappy, and it's an awful lot more fun to be that way.

But here's what's changing: Where advertising used to work, where mass media - sprayin' and prayin' - used to work was for the great, unwashed pit of mediocrity there in the middle of extremely good and extremely bad.

Everybody who was just kind of okay, who wasn't noteworthy or remarkable in any way, shape or form, they just went about their job. They thought they did okay. They went home, lathered, rinsed, and repeated like an army of zombies for the rest of their life.

This is what's becoming less and less effective by the second. It's getting ignored.

Yankelovich & Sons, a marketing research firm, last year found that the average person in a major city hears a certain number of messages every day.

How many messages do you think that is, each of us hears every day, approximately?

5,000!

That's your number. 5,000 messages yammering on and on in there in the middle that nobody remembers.

A company that can provide truly shareworthy service will begin to decrease their advertising budget. If you do this right, the marketing budget will continue to go up. Advertising down, marketing up.

Where are we going to spend that money in the gap?

On your staff. On the answers to their questions they'll be answering in the next week.

So why is bad customer service so dangerous?

Let me share something that my partner, Roy, wrote about in his *Wall Street Journal* Business Book of the Year, *Secret Formulas of The Wizard of Ads*:

An in-depth study conducted by Technical Assistance Research Programs, T.A.R.P., of Washington D.C., uncovered some things I think you should know.

Number one: On average, twenty-six unhappy customers won't complain for every one that will.

Number two: Yet each of these unhappy twenty-seven customers will tell an average of sixteen other people about his or her bad experience with your firm.

Number three: This means every complaint you hear represents 432 negative impressions. How many people should have to complain before you take action to permanently remedy your problem? By the time you hear a particular complaint three times, the problem has been mentioned to an average of 1296 people.

Number four: It costs five times as much to attract a new customer as it costs to keep an old one.

Number five: ninety-one percent of your unhappy customers will never buy from you again.

And Number six: But if you make a focused effort to remedy your customer's complaints, eighty-two percent of them will stay with you.

Steve Tuschmidt, the owner of Mid-America Harley Davidson said something that has stuck with me since I heard him say it, "Eventually everybody is going to stub their toe. It's how you fix it that matters." And that's really true.

So I'm not asking for the impossible, I'm not challenging you to do the impossible today - which is to always be perfect. Just make a conscious effort to figure out what you can do to make things right if something does go badly.

Now, back to the questions for your staff:

What would you have do to deliver shareworthy customer service? What would you have to do to cause someone to get onto Facebook, to pick up the phone, to send an email to our company and say "Holy crap, that was amazing"? What would you have to do? What could you do that someone would share?

Are you familiar with talkshow host and financial planner Dave Ramsey? I'm a big fan of Dave Ramsey.

Ramsey wrote this in his book, *EntreLeadership*, on small business:

I'm known for telling people to deliver pizzas or throw papers for some quick extra money. I had an energetic and analytical young man working for our team during the day, but he wanted some more money so he decided to deliver pizzas.

Anyone can just walk up to the door and hand someone a pizza. But John was not content with doing just the basic process, because his best money came from the tips.

Was he doing because it made him feel good? No, he was doing it to make extra money. If he gave better service, he made more money; there was a direct correlation.

Took the exact same amount of effort. He probably was happier and enjoyed it more, and went home happier at the end of the night. But he wasn't doing it for that he was doing it for money.[1]

Read the chapter. Ramsey gives a few examples of what John did that will totally rock your socks.

And then tells you how management let John down.

Leadership is required to win in business.

Next question: If we had a contest to reward legendary customer service, how would we measure it? Because if we do have this contest, y'all have to be the ones to decide the rules and how it works.

That's right. Your employees need to decide the parameters. They need to own it. You have the right to arbitrate it, but they have to develop it themselves.

Do you understand? This is critical. If it's going to work and be sustainable, it needs to be *their* program.

Last question:

What do you need from us? What do you need from management and ownership? What resources do you need from us to provide this legendary customer service?

How can you help them?

Another way to say that is:

What legendary, shareworthy service do you demand from the owners of this company?

Advertising is not the future of the growth of your company.

Not advertising, not raw, spray-and-pray advertising.

Systems, policies, and procedures - the things that are shareworthy - are what's going to continue to grow your company, and it's in your company's hands.

You are part of the marketing department. Your whole team is part of the marketing department.

If you had a contest to reward and measure legendary customer service, what would you do?

That's what you would like to hear from your team when they answer those questions by next week.

That's the key to future, sustainable success for your company.

Meeting adjourned.

[1]*Ramsey, Dave (2011-09-20). EntreLeadership (pp. 109-110). Simon & Schuster, Inc.. Kindle Edition.*

41. IT'S BEEN ONE WEEK

I'm at the office of my oldest and dearest client, Chapman Heating & Cooling, one week after they presented those questions to their employees.

What follows in a transcript of my meeting with the owners.

TIM: Here's what I think; you've got all those things back. Now you have to talk. One of you in this room has to talk, to each person who turned one in. Ask them about what they wrote - their dreams and ideal vacations and big boy toys. OK you wrote down a rifle? Tell me about it.

Just so they know that you've heard them. Just so they understand that, okay, this wasn't something that we just had you fill out, rah-rah, let's go back to doing the same things we've always done.

Ask them if they have any thoughts already that they've written down about what we can do to improve, what to cut - legendary customer service.

Shouldn't take more than ten minutes per employee. It's really important to do.

And then you're gonna tell them, OK over the next week all I want you to do is be mindful through the course of your day and your week of your interactions with customers.

What could you do differently? What could you do better?

What did you do awesomely that made you think, "Hey, we could make this into a policy or a procedure."

That's what you're leading toward - systems, policies, and procedures. Things that are measurable. Things that can be duplicated. Things that are spreadsheet-worthy.

Spreadsheet-worthy service. Doesn't have the same ring to it.

Then, next week you're going to have another twenty minute meeting with them, and maybe this will be a group meeting, and you hand out sheets of, "OK here are these fourteen facets of shareworthy service."

OK, what would privilege look like? Privilege is making someone feel special. "Hey, we don't tell everybody this, but we'll let you in behind the ropes." How could we do privilege in our business? In our company? How could we utilize memory in our company?

They may not have the answers, but maybe they do. I would first ask them to do it individually, and that's a sheer answer cause you never know where the circles might overlap, and then do it together as a group.

This all happens in a period of about two weeks. It costs them nothing except a little bit of time in their mornings.

But you start with talking a little bit with them about their rewards so they're reminded that this is a means to an end.

You're not gonna buy every one of them an RV or a camper, but you're listening.

You're all thinking: "How can we all get to [big hairy goal]."

That's the goal. I just got goosebumps saying it, but that's the goal.

PHIL: With the same number of people.

TIM: Yes! Bingo! That's what I think this could do. And so you sit down with them and go over the worksheet with the fourteen facets, and then starting second quarter we're going to have a contest.

But they have to define the rules of the contest. You have a final say but no one is more qualified to determine what the contest should be and how it should be measured than those guys.

And then the contest, and this is so crucial, has to have a big carrot at the end of the stick. But it also has to have little carrots along the way.

Even as simple as a discount card for [local pizza joint] Shakespeare's or here's this or here's that. Some little thing. Little incremental rewards and then a big payout at the end.

And I don't know if that's annually, again, I just love since you're a seasonal business, do it the first day of every season.

And again it's measurable. It's not measurable tomorrow, but my gosh, it could be sustainable. It could be something that three years from now it's like we never even realized. And then think about it, it makes an awful lot of sense.

I'm not saying that it's right but I am saying that it's logical. That this practice of empowering your employees to be your marketing department to make them realize and be rewarded for being in your marketing department?

Heck, what could it hurt? We know direct mail's not working.

And it's not working anywhere. It's not working in California, it's not working in Tennessee, and I think that you focus your marketing budget on things where we can tell stories.

Systems, policies and procedures. But those are going to come from the guys. Or from you. Or from Heidi at the front desk. Those are going to come from people who are paying attention, who are mindful.

It starts with mindfulness.

And again, even if it doesn't show an increase in our top line in the first quarter, everybody is working together toward a common goal.

And that common goal is to make customers freakin' dazzled by us. I would wait to start a big referral program until October.

That's really it. It's not complicated.

There are two ways you could kind of fall off the balance beam. On one side, you go all woo-woo, happy, no measurement, let's just feel good. Then the feel good will start to fade. Then it's done and you go back to doing what you always did. Or, falling off the other side, it's so top-down that they don't feel like they have any control or input in it.

Then they're just following orders and they actually resent it, and it will blow up in your face. It has got to be grassroots. It has got to be bottom up. They have to feel like they are being listened to, and they have to feel like they are a part of it. And they constantly have to be re-reminded that there are carrots at the end of the stick.

HEIDI: We're buying into their ideas. All their ideas.

SHANA: I think the key word is empowering.

RON: A guy named Tim (meaning me) here in town sent me an email the other day. It was talking about Walt Disney and what Disney does right.

TIM: Thank you so much. I have a follow-up too. You guys were perfect for this.

Disney said, "Out of all the things I've said, the most vital is coordinating those who work with me and aiming their efforts at a certain goal."

Walt Disney, one of the most powerful men in the world at his time, didn't say "work for me" he said "work with me." He didn't care about taking all the credit.

That's why I think this could work. You guys have always been like this. From the first day I sat down with you, it wasn't just lip service.

You actually believe this stuff.

Now it's a matter of systemizing it. The success or failure of this program hinges on our ability to measure and reward it, not to just make everybody feel good. Because it will fail, and fail quickly. And then we've just wasted time. And I don't want that to happen.

You know where I thought this could actually work?

When I'm looking at Levi that morning last week at your annual meeting. He's looking at your business plan. And, Nathan, you're up there at the front of the room explaining how you arrived at the goals. You guys, you actually believe this stuff. You actually share it with your guys. They're going to be pointed in the same direction you are. And I thought, okay, maybe this will work.

Again direct mail is not working, right? Worse case scenario? Everybody comes together. That can't be a bad thing.

This is a pilot program. Well, no. You're my proving ground and I'm yours. I mean we're both kind of in this together.

RON: The other exciting thing to me is that it's not new. Other companies have been doing this sort of thing in other industries.

TIM: Right. Disney's been doing it. It's not new. It's just hard. It's hard if you aren't willing to do the different. It's uncomfortable. It involves letting go of some control and being very transparent. You guys already do all those things. This is actually the easy part, but a lot of companies will say, "Oh, that won't work," and they'll never try it.

HEIDI: I think it's also critical that we stay on the beam, and we stay moving with it. Sometimes we become stagnant or comfortable and that's what hurts us.

TIM: Yeah, what if we get two weeks of finally ten degree weather and boom, we're busy? That's okay. If we've got to run calls all day we've got to run calls all day but it's your and my job to keep the bus moving. Really and truly. You are the new chief customer experience officer. CCEO. Pepsi actually has that.

There are worse ways to feel about coming to work in the morning to than a company, who, if you deliver legendary service, is going to reward you for it.

Again, there are worse ways to spend the day - especially when it's hot. Like, I'm thinking it's 110 degrees out there and you're sweating and you're working overtime and your mindful of, "Okay, how can I make these people feel awesome?"

Because there's something in it for me in the end, and there's something in it for all of us at the end. [Big hairy goal]. I couldn't stop thinking about that number the other day, watching Levi - feeling like he was a part of something. That's a big deal. It really is a family here. So many people say that and they don't mean it.

The next step would be for me to list out these steps for you and share them with you. And then you would schedule meetings with everybody just to talk about what they wrote. Again, no more than ten minutes each and there's absolutely no residual benefit from it. You won't see an immediate benefit from having that talk. It's like diet and exercise. It's like training for a marathon. You're not ready. You don't go run two miles one day and then the marathon is the next. That's exactly what this is like. I think, I have no idea, I've never trained for a marathon. Total hypocrite.

HEIDI: Okay, what about not everybody turning these in?

NATHAN: I've been thinking about that because I'm sure they didn't. How many? Ballpark? How many didn't?

PHIL: Did you get eighty percent?

TIM: That's remarkable to me.

HEIDI: Eighty percent is good?

TIM: That's incredible. That's a home run.

You go to them one by one and you say we're still waiting on you. Why didn't we get it? Look them in the eye. Don't be mean but...

HEIDI: Hold them accountable?

TIM: Yeah. We meant it. This is not lip service.

SHANA: We want your thoughts.

PHIL: What? Is there anything I can do to help you talk through them? We need them by Friday or Tuesday, whatever. Not an email.

RON: They've never thought about those kinds of questions before.

TIM: Exactly. Do you remember the dream manager? Most of the employees, their dreams were small because no one had ever asked them that question before. They didn't even think it was even possible to do this stuff and so it was like, "My dream to just have my checkbook balanced."

TIM: You all need to follow up. I think it's important that you all take a role in that, that's it's not... I mean ultimately there's going to be one person with an inbox, that's you. But you can do that perfectly within the scope of your time frame. I think it's important that everybody start to set appointments. Ask where the other ones are. Is there anything I can do to help you?

You don't even have to say we're very serious about this. In fact, don't stay that. Show them. By asking you will show that you are serious about this.

That's the first step. That's all we need to know, Heidi.

We don't need to eat the elephant in one bite. Just one bite at a time, and the next step is to start setting appointments with the people who did turn them in. That also lights a fire under the people who didn't turn them in because they will talk.

PHIL: Just let them know that we're still open to accept them.

TIM: If this works, you'll never have a problem with recruitment again. There will be a line out your door.

Get them all in. Start visiting them. Again, go through their answers. It's a feedback loop. It's like okay we got them, let's just talk about them. At the end of that meeting ask them over the next week to be mindful of their workday. Where could you, you know, where are opportunities for kindness and professionalism? You have to start getting them oriented to think about it, and it doesn't happen over night.

PHIL: In the ten minute meeting, going over this, that's when you ask them to be mindful?

TIM: Yeah, at the end of that. Next week, be mindful of kindness and professionalism. Where are opportunities? What are things you're already doing that others could do? We're looking for things that could become systems, policies, and procedures. And we should have two types of advertising moving forward. We should have systems, policies, procedures, straightforward pricing, job and family guarantee, and people who go bug nuts crazy about how wonderful we are.

Okay. One last thing. You guys had talked about wanting to go visit a heating and air conditioning company. I have a different idea that I want to run by you.

I want us to go to Disney ...

42. A CALL FROM THE SHAREWORTHY HALL OF FAME

I hate automated phone trees.

Actually, do you know anyone who's ever said in the history of ever: "Gee. I love automated phone trees."

It is my great wish to never press '1' for anything again.

(No, those automated things where you have to pretend they're real and hope the voice recognition software picks up what you're saying don't count. In fact, I think they're worse.)

I love Ruby. (Almost as much as we love Emma ... but that's a different story for a different day ... it's kind of complicated.)

Don't worry. My wife loves Ruby, too.

Ruby Receptionists out of Portland, Oregon.

receptionists

A quirky, quizzical and ... umm ... qualified company, that became our amazing virtual receptionists last week. In an effort to protect our company's most important assets: our time, focus, energy and enthusiasm, we've put in a series of policies and procedures to help us help our customers and not-for-profit friends a little more.

Anyway, at the end of our introductory orientation call, Kendra from Ruby Receptionists asked:

"You're all set! Is there we can get for you today, Tim?"

I joked, "How about a puppy?"

Fast forward five days.

A package from Ruby arrives at our front door.

Kendra listened.

(Sarah Choo-Choo said we should name the puppy Ruff. Two-year-olds always get naming rights.)

43. THE SECRETS OF THE GIFT ARTISTS

Do you give great gifts? Perfect gifts? Are you that person?

Each of us has that at least one person in our world who's just a better gift-giver than everyone else. They make a high art out of giving just the right gift.

That's a powerful skill to possess, my friends.

I asked a couple Gift Artists in my life to share their secrets with you.

My Amazing Sister, Lynn:

1. **Always remember what you are really giving is love and affection.**

Narrow your custom gift list to those closest to you and key in on their passions, interests or personality. Keep these things in mind throughout your travels and adventures all year long.

Cramming Christmas shopping into one day or weekend or even month will not yield the thoughtful gifts you desire to give.

For others, buy cool stuff in bulk. Johnson and Johnson makes a lavender lotion that they sell at Target for $.99. It promises to "melt away stress and help you unwind and feel at ease." Jackpot! I bought twenty of those and keep them in my desk drawer for when a coworker is having a stressful day.

Put it in cellophane and tie with a nice ribbon (see #4)!

2. Imagine how you want the recipient to feel when they open the gift.

Oh, that's nice, or Oh, my goodness! I can't believe you did this! Go the extra mile to make that happen.

When the perfect gift for our parents was an October maple tree they admired at the neighbors house, I realized that a tree in December might not have much impact.

But when we all worked together to write on fifty paper maple leaves what we had learned or appreciated about them, it became much more impactful.

3. You don't have to spend a lot.

My kids like their stocking stuffers better than big gifts. In fact we don't give big gifts anymore.

The joy we share opening socks and underwear and fake mustaches and fair trade coffee on Christmas morning, much outweighs a pair of Uggs or an electric guitar.

They work to earn money for those big items throughout the year, giving those things more meaning too.

4. Wrapping tricks – develop your style, keep it simple and use quality products.

I never buy curling ribbon or stick on bows.

I buy fabric ribbon – preferably wired edged – only. It makes everything look better and you can get it cheap on sale.

Other tricks – clear cellophane bags. But even a tea bag in one of those with a nice ribbon and you can give your assistant a gift of relaxation in a lovely package.

I also never buy holiday gift tags, but make my own. You can buy all kinds of inexpensive craft papers now that make this easy.

The message that accompanies the gift is important; with creative gift giving you sometimes have to explain why you got something for someone.

For holidays, I use only two or three patterns of gift wrap in the same color scheme and mix it up from year to year.

5. **I have an amazing partner who executes my crazy ideas.**

I am research and development; he is engineering and accounting.

If I say, "You-know-what would make a good gift for so and so," he will track it down and find it at the best price.

We're a pretty formidable team.

6. **I like people to like what I give them.**

I like packages to be beautiful and admired.

I don't have the time I used to to devote to those things and it makes me a little sad.

When someone gives you a gift that makes you feel special and loved, it's a wonderful thing!

Oh and one last thing, *appreciate beautiful wrapping and thoughtful gifts when you are the receiver.*

Don't let it make you feel guilty or jealous. Some people just love to do it.

Calling someone Martha Stewart in those circumstances is generally not a compliment.

My partner, copywriting genius, and best buddy, Ryan:

I've never really thought of it as a process. I just buy nice things because, unlike my cousin, I'm not talented enough to make anything cool.

The best tip I can give is: *Listen.*

The more you listen to conversations with people or read their posts on Facebook, the more you learn about what interests them. If I know I'll be buying a gift for that person in the foreseeable future, I'll make a mental (or actual) note.

Then, when I'm online or at the store, I may see something that brings that person to mind.

I usually find these things online. If I'm buying for someone local, I remind myself that they have friends and relatives living nearby who also know their tastes, so I try to avoid buying them something from the local store that might also be bought for them by someone else.

A simple search on Google or Amazon will give you a plethora of gift ideas. Find one that you think will knock their socks off and buy it. The more unique, the better.

Another tip...bookmark pages throughout the year.

If I'm online in April and I see a potential gift for someone, I'll bookmark the site in a special "gift" category so I can review it later.

Right now, I'm finding pages that I bookmarked six months ago that I completely forgot about. But I'm so glad I took five seconds to do it...because it's making my Christmas shopping a bit easier.

Why do I enjoy it?

Good question. I'm not sure. I guess I like going back to people's homes and seeing the gift I gave them on display. I love remarks like "where did you get this?" or "how did you know I'd like this?" I'd like to think that when they look at it throughout the year, they think of our friendship in a positive way.

Mushy enough for ya?

Yep. Perfectly Mushy. Ryan got me this for my most recent birthday, shortly after the passing of Steve Jobs.

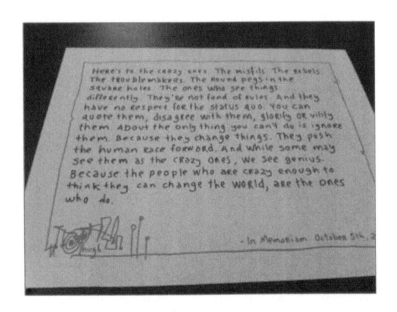

44. "SAW THIS. THOUGHT OF YOU."

A gift to you: Five of my favorite words.

Is there anything more exciting than when someone shares something expressly with you?

That someone was thinking about you when you weren't (necessarily) thinking of them?

Share stuff.

45. DEE P. NAMES THE LOBSTERS

Ever hear of naming the lobsters?

You go to a seafood restaurant with one of those big lobster tanks by the front door. Your kid starts naming them, and suddenly you can't eat one.

They have names. They're now more than a market price dinner. They're cute little Disney creatures with names and families and hijinks and adventures.

Your kid just kept you from eating that lobster because your kid made it a little more real.

Dee Pontious at Jansen's Heating & Air taught me how to name the lobsters for companies.

I first saw the poster middle of last year. It was 24" x 36" brightly colored poster board covered with rifles and the lights of Vegas and boats and grills. They were surrounding a big number.

"What's that?" I asked Dee.

"Well, I wanted everyone on the team to realize we all won if we hit our company goal this year, so I had everybody go through and cut out their dream toy if we got our profit sharing bonus.

"I had them think about, imagine, then make the effort to cut out what they wanted.

"We all had to paste them on this poster here, and then I put it up by the back door so it was the first thing everyone saw when they arrived in the morning and the last thing they saw before they went home at night."

It's not the first contest Dee's done brilliantly. It seems every time I go there to visit, she's got them all involved in some new scavenger hunt or bingo or team competition.

Dee Pontious is a genius. She's not the only one there at the shop.

Coincidentally, Jansen's Heating & Air was named contractor of the year by their trade association.

46. BEST BUY MADE MY MOM CRY

Prior to last week, I've known my mom to cry only three times: at the funeral for each of her parents and on February 13, 2010 – the day she realized she'd been putting up with my dad for fifty years.

I kid!

Seriously, though – mom's not a crier. She's kind, hard-working, helpful, thoughtful, volunteers at a local food pantry, reads books, cooks and gardens. She is not technically savvy. She does not cry.

Last week, Best Buy made my mom cry.

Is it any wonder reports of their slow demise litter the inter webs?

Okay, technically the corporation didn't make my mom cry. Trish did.

Just like when any company's employee or employees make a mistake, it wasn't the fault of the entire company. In nearly every case, one rude idiot launches 1,000 words (406 in mine).

Trish – in the Geek Squad – at the Champaign, Illinois location. I'm not redacting her last name to be polite. I just don't know it. If I did, I'd include it, along with her home phone, address, social security number, PIN #, blood type and known allergies.

After years of good customer service with Geek Squad – and a very pleasant and apologetic follow-up from someone else after Poop Face Trish (PFT) brought my mom to tears – it only took one bad experience for mom to tell me and for me to tell you.

Appropriately, I'm delivering a talk to one of my client's company meetings about what it takes to perform legendary customer service.

Guess what little anecdote I'm starting with to put them in the right frame of mind?

But, what my client may not yet know, is that legendary customer service has a whole lot more to do with the employer than the employees.

As Roy used to say, "A fish stinks from the head down."

Oh, and Poop Face Trish?

If I find out where you live, I'm putting spiders in your bed.

47. THE URINAL GNAT

A friend came to me yesterday to express her frustrations.

Work had her down, done, and all out.

We broke down and isolated her great, all-consuming irritants and found them, really, to be nothing more than urinal gnats.

Guys know. Guys who either used to live in less-than-HGTV-worthy homes when they were younger or who frequented less-than-fancy bars when they were there yesterday know.

The urinal gnats hover in the john around said receptacles. They never land. They never bite you and leave red, stinging welts in your nether-regions that make you want to cry.

They won't give you the Asian flu, rickets, or ADHD.

Even a urinal gnat with the most cranky disposition on its worst day does nothing more than float there giving you something to look at while you keep your eyes front, thank you.

But, in your mind, you can allow urinal gnats to grow to prodigious horse-flies that buzz like chain-saws – disrupting your disruption with their menacing tendency to land and grab hold of something.

Same is true of my friend.

Her problems were no more than a small series of inconveniences in an otherwise pretty good job. Most everyone loves and respects her. She's good at what she does.

It happens to all of us.

But if you don't communicate ... if you let the pool of problems fester in the heat and humidity of your workplace ... they can buzz over the sacred dividing line and creep into my – your co-worker's – urinal.

Or, worse, a customer's.

Your customer doesn't really care all that much if you're having a bad day. They don't care if you've answered their question 273 times already today. They've come to you wanting to buy from you, and there will either be a connect or disconnect between you and them that happens almost imperceptibly in the first three seconds of your time together.

So, if you have real problems, fix them away from the other patrons, please.

If you have a few small inconveniences, though, just don't forget to flush and wash your hands of them before returning to work.

Don't make mountains out of molehills.

Don't make horseflies out of urinal gnats.

And, please, tip your bartenders and waitresses ... provided they've washed their hands.

48. THE LOVE OF A LIFETIME CUSTOMER

Read a simple-but-startling angle this morning on customer value.

Have you calculated what a customer's worth over the course of her lifetime?

What if – just one time – you calculated your marketing budget off that amount?

In *Embracing Lifetime Value*, Seth Godin suggests this simple challenge:

So, a chiropractor might see a new patient being worth $2,500, easily. And yet... how much is she spending on courting, catering to and seducing that new customer? My guess is that $50 feels like a lot to the doc. Instead of comparing what you invest to the benefit you receive from the first bill, the first visit, the first transaction, it's important to not only recognize but embrace the true lifetime value of one more customer.

Write it down. Post it on the wall. What would happen if you spent 100% of that amount on each of your next ten new customers? That's more money than you have to spend right now, I know that, but what would happen? Imagine how fast you would grow, how quickly the word would spread.

Do this as an exercise.

What if you spent just as he suggested? You've suddenly got an influx of cash to invest in tickling the delighted fancy of customer after customer. What might you do?

What might you do differently than you were planning to do?

In brainstorming and strategic planning, we often use the "what if money were no object" parameter to loosen mental impediments and objections. Here, it's the same thing, but we're putting faces to that parameter – beautiful, evangelical faces. What would you do?

Because from these ideas, you might pare some small derivative that would never otherwise have come to you. You might find five. Heck, you might realize ten brand new unique-to-you ideas for some serious fancy-tickling just because you stopped to think differently about the value of your customers.

So, answer me these questions three, 'ere the other side you'll see:

1. Do you really understand how much a customer is worth over her lifetime?

2. Why is #1 important?

3. When are you scheduling your planning session to do something differently next year as a result of #1 and #2?

Do it this week, please. Or don't.

49. A LOCAL BUSINESS WAKE-UP CALL

Do you like the idea of supporting local businesses?

Is that like asking a politician if he's for more jobs and against crime?

But ... and it's an awfully big BUT ... your locally-owned business has got to meet me MORE than halfway. Sorry if that seems unfair. Heck, it is unfair.

Get over it.

One local restaurant urges folks to get on board to help them beat the chains. "Chains are bad. We are good." That sorta thing.

To wit:

Twice, I called for delivery and was greeted with "hello?"

Both times, it sounded kind of like I was bothering them by trying to offer them money.

I asked if I was, indeed, calling the restaurant. Both times, I was greeted with a self-righteous, "yeah."

The second time, I was abruptly cut off twice when asking simple questions.

Neither time did the phone person say "thank you" or "good bye." Each time, they simply hung up.

Help you beat the chains? Help yourself.

Meanwhile …

One of those nasty chains – Target – answered the phone at not one, but two different stores in two different towns by nicely saying,

"Hello, this is Target. What can I help you find today?"

That's right. A real, live, human being person answered. No automated phone tree. Also no hangups or entitled, snippy, self-righteousness.

Target obviously had a system in place. How exactly was that evil? That's like calling kittens evil.

Your locally-owned business has got to meet me more than halfway.

Or you'll lose.

It's not a temporary inconvenience. It's the new reality of your business, and you best embrace it and – more importantly – develop chain-like, repeatable systems to do it better.

Remember, in this age and day, whether you deliver an exceptionally good or bad experience, social media will only accelerate the inevitable.

I want to celebrate our independents. I really do. I'm sure you feel the same way to one degree or another.

Help me, please.

"Thank you."

50. CONSISTENCY & DEPENDABILITY

"I'm a liar."

One of my clients said this to me a few weeks ago. It lit the shareworthy service fire (Best Buy making my mom cry just poured kerosene on it).

He voices his own ads on the radio. He frequently talks about what customers can expect when they do business with us. He'd received a couple less-than-stellar reviews of his service team.

"If I'm there on the radio saying one thing ... and we're doing another ... well, I'm a liar."

What a moment. What a frightening, enlightening step-on-a-rake moment of clarity.

As consumers, we've grown so accustomed to being underwhelmed and mistrustful of advertising that we're not even surprised anymore – in fact, we assume it's the norm – when a company's long on talk and short on action.

Not my client. We've launched a program to measure and reward improvement in our service.

It's sad that consistency and dependability are facets of shareworthy service, but they most certainly are.

The best way to generate shareworthy service?

Disappoint a customer.

You have to raise the bar with systems, policies and procedures that spell out each interaction with a customer. Your team has to know what is expected of them – every time.

A Big Mac should taste the same whether you eat it in your hometown or Walton-on-Thames. Why? Because we sleep better at night knowing that, whether we even like them or not, certain things are always consistent.

Can you say the same about your company?

Are you saying one thing with your advertising and delivering another?

All the time?

It's okay if you can't. It's an opportunity.

Dependability – Can we count on your company to deliver what you say you will when you say you will?

Consistency – Every single time? Without fail? Consistency is the dependability of your dependability.

Sure, we all make mistakes. My rock-solid dependable email marketing company had a server failure recently, and they didn't send my Daily Blur email at 5:00 AM like always.

They apologized.

They fixed the problem quickly.

They followed up with me to let me know it had been fixed.

And then followed up again to say they forwarded my thank you note around the office and it made everyone's day.

My email marketing company fixed it.

My client is fixing what needs fixed.

How about you?

(It's about this time in Hazzard County that I should mention the only dangerous thing for you at this point is that if you don't know ... then you best get to findin' out, bub.)

51. THE PIT OF MEDIOCRITY

We've covered the bad. We've covered the exceptional.

That's the thing about extremes: for better and worse, they get covered. And even when a company stinks up the place, they usually get at least one chance to make good – and that chance, if taken advantage of, tends to get as much coverage as the offense. We do love our redemptions, don't we?

But what about the rest?

Ugh.

Imagine an inverted bell curve.

At both extremes, you get discussed.

Everyone else – wallowing in the pit of average – gets ignored.

Wait ... here ... I'll draw it on a legal pad for you.

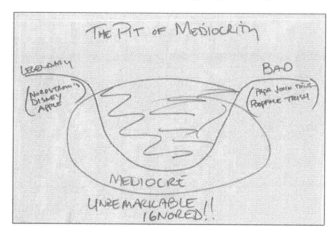

Breathtaking, I admit.

There – in the saggy, soggy bottom sits a black hole suck from which it's hard to escape. I mean, why would you try to escape when you don't think there's a problem?

"Our service is fine."

"We do a pretty good job."

"Hey, we're good. When we make a mistake, we always try to fix it."

Fish don't know they're in water.

It's a dangerous wasteland, my friends. It's a narcotic malaise that deadens souls of employees, companies, and customers.

And it's true for most of the companies with whom we do business, isn't it?

52. INTERNING AT DISNEY - TWENTY YEARS LATER

"Dump your ice cream cone on accident on Main Street? Tell them. You'll get a new one. Offering to take a picture of your family so you can be in it? They do it all the time."

My friend, fellow pinball fanatic and former biology lab partner Suzanne interned at Disney a ... umm ... uhh ... a while ago. :)

It's still with her. I can't tell it any better than this:

Yes, years after interning there, I am still brainwashed.

I still point with two fingers or the whole hand.

I still offer to take pictures of families I see out and about (which drives my husband NUTS!), but it was so part of the culture there.

I think that's the difference. Customer service has to be part of the culture.

We were told over and over again that we were the face of Disney and it didn't matter if that guest (yes GUEST, not customer – a tidbit that Target adopted after sending their management folks through Disney training) was in our parks for the tenth time or first time, our job was to make it feel like their first time and make it wonderful.

Nine great things could have happened to them on their trip, but guests (customers) don't talk about that.

They talk about the ONE BAD thing that happened. It was drilled into us to NOT be the one bad thing.

That said, I interned there when I was twenty. Those principals have stuck with me throughout my career, even though it's been in high tech — not tourism.

Thanks, Suz.

In 250 words ... Suzanne covers twelve of the fourteen facets of shareworthy service.

Disney, dude.

All these years later, Mouse can still bring it.

53. FRANCIS, JAKE, AND CARRABBA'S

Francis Pass is my client and my friend. He is also on the Mt. Rushmore of storytellers. We got to talking about shareworthy service the other day, and I was able to record – and have transcribed – his story of a recent legendarily magnificently delightful dinner he shared with his wife Patricia and a young man named Jake.

Take it away, Francis:

Patricia and I were in Sarasota, Florida. We saw the sign for Carrabba's. We had been seeing the advertisements on national TV and had never been to a Carrabba's.

So we went to Carrabba's and we got this young man named Jake.

Right off the bat the hostess seats us and then Jake comes over and he introduced himself as all waiters do: "I'm Jake and I'm going to be taking care of you." But Jake went above and beyond that.

He extended his hand out to me and said, "And you are?" And I said I was Francis.

"And this is your lovely date?" And so Patricia then extended her hand because he knew the proper etiquette – only shake a lady's hand when she extends it. So she shook his hand.

"And your last name?" Pass, I said.

"Francis and Patricia Pass," he said. "Well, I'm Jake. I'm going to be taking care of you this evening. Have you ever been here with us before?"

No, as a matter of fact, Jake, this is our first time ever to go to a Carrabba's. "Wow. Okay," he said. "I want this to be a fantastic event for you, and I'm going to make sure that you have a wonderful experience. I'll do everything I can to do that for you. Would you like something from the bar?" Patricia and I said we wanted wine.

Jake said, "Do you know what you might like?"

And I said to Jake, "I haven't even looked at your wine list." Jake said, "I'm going to go get your water, and I'll be back out."

So when he came back I showed him what I thought. He said it was an excellent choice. He disappears and he brings back this beautiful, blonde-headed girl. And he brings her over to our table, literally, and says "Francis, Patricia, this is Sheila. She's an outstanding wine glass server. She's brought your glasses for this evening and then she'll be bringing back the wine, and I just wanted you to meet this young lady."

Then he turned to her and says "Sheila, this is Francis and Patricia Pass and this is their first time here, but it's also their first time ever at a Carrabba's. We want to make this a special event for them."

Of course she was grinning from ear to ear. Well, she gives us our glasses and then the wine comes, and they're gently poured. They start off with Patricia's first and then poured mine.

Then, during the course there's this young lady going around to all the tables with this little roller vacuum. Jake gets her by the arm and brings her over and says "Lisa, I'd like to introduce you to Francis and Patricia Pass. Lisa is our most fantastic floor cleaner." Then he made absolutely certain that she was aware this was a first-time event.

This was when I began to kind of look at the people around us. The table to the left, table to the right, and every time Jake would show up they'd now stop what they were doing and they'd look and they'd listen. He's not taking care of their tables, okay? And I could tell by expressions, they were like "What the heck's going on? Who are these people?" You know what I mean?

The whole evening went that way, and when he brought my meal out, he brought out this other little bowl. I had not ordered soup because I had the salad. Jake says "You know, Francis, the dish that you ordered is made with a champagne cream sauce. It's excellent, but it is more on the bland side," and he said, "I can tell from the wine you ordered, and the salad you had that it might be just a little too bland, so I brought this sauce so that if it's too bland, spoon a little on it." He says, "Patricia, you might like this also because it's more like your sauce. But if you want more..."

And I did want more! It was a great recommendation. The whole event was just – it was the best legendary restaurant service we've ever received, anywhere.

After dinner I asked Jake if he had ever considered a position in sales, and he said, "You know, I've been told that before."

I gave him my business card, and I told him if he ever made it to Illinois to come see me, and I would create a position for him – period!

And then I told Jake I wanted to recommend him to our franchise – One Hour Heating & Air Conditioning – right there in Sarasota.

And Jake said, "That'd be fantastic. I'm twenty-eight years old, and I need to get a real job."

It was the most unbelievable service I've ever had in my life. I think our bill was $87. I gave him a $35 tip.

Thanks, Francis!

Multiply that times ten tables a night, five nights a week. Heck, ole' Jake might be taking a pay cut going to work for One Hour. :)

And to think – Jake wasn't there one minute longer than any other server working that night. He didn't have any special tools that any other server couldn't have used as well. He just chose to have more fun and be more interesting to and interested in his tables. And he made forty percent while others, no doubt, whined and complained and wondered why Jake was so lucky getting all the good tippers while they got their measly ten to twenty percent.

How about you? Do you remember your last legendary customer service experience?

54. PRIVILEGE AT CAP CITY FINE DINER

I'm in Columbus, Ohio, where I'm in the middle of eating the best fried chicken dinner of my life.

I'm a guest of a delightful Christian radio station – 104.9 The River. My hosts have quickly become friends.

I passed on the meatloaf my three dinner companions at the Cap City Fine Diner all ordered. They assure me it's the signature dish.

Three bites into my chicken, I assure them they're wrong.

The general manager comes up to our table to introduce himself to our table. Always a nice touch, right, but not all that uncommon?

He asks of our meals. I tell him his fried chicken dinner is stupid.

I mean it's good. I'm hip that way. At least my son thinks so. Still.

I tell him I'm from out-of-town and my three friends said we absolutely had to visit this place while I was there. He thanked them and wondered if we were going to try the signature dessert: The Cup of Chocolate.

"It's a large mug," he said, "filled with warm, gooey chocolate lava cake, topped with vanilla bean ice cream and hot fudge."

"Mbmbm phgmm," I replied, on bite seventeen of my fried chicken dinner.

"But," he continued, "and we don't put this on the menu, but our regulars order it with warm peanut butter between the lava cake and the ice cream."

"Now you're just showing off," I said (borrowing one of my favorite phrases from my friend, Scotty).

He smiled, clearly proud of his place and his food, and wished us an enjoyable rest of our dinner and thanked us for coming.

"They do that a lot here," Bill said at our table, "I know there are several things you can order off the menu."

"Like at In and Out Burger," said Craig.

"Yep. Same thing," I said, and as I was about to continue to talk about what a delight it can be to be in the know and rewarded and made to feel special by knowing things 'outsiders' don't, our waiter arrived at our table.

"A gift," he said, "from us. You could have gone to a lot of places during your short time here."

A giant, steaming Cup O' Chocolate. Four spoons.

And peanut butter, of course.

I was a regular now, after all.

There's a video of this legendary dessert at www.GoodCompanyStuff.com.

Watch at your hunger's peril.

55. JUST ONE QUICK APPLE STORY - TWICE

When I was doing my scholarly Facebook research on shareworthy service stories, my old friend Amy shared a juicy Apple story from her husband. It's ... just ... so ... cool.

Yes, I am an unapologetic Apple fanboy. But there are reasons I'm an unapologetic fanboy. This is one of them. Take it away, Amy's husband:

Last December I purchased an iPad at my local Target. At first it was "off limits" to my two kids (Pete is six and Tessa is three), but over time my wife and I relaxed that stance and both kids play with it - sometimes with less than ideal supervision. That was the case on Monday morning. Pete likes to get a few sessions of Angry Birds in on his way to school. On Monday, he walked out the door with the iPad in one hand and his backpack in the other. While fortunately he's more coordinated than his father, he wasn't able to successfully get both the iPad and the backpack to the car on this morning---coming back into the house with a concerned look on his face. The iPad had hit the driveway and apparently landed right on the glass screen, creating a large spider-web break. Bummer!! (Although, truthfully, I'm not sure that was the word I used).

I knew there were a number of places that specialized in iPad/iPhone repairs, but had concerns about potentially voiding my warranty by using someone other than Apple. I am typically cheap, but wanted to make the best decision, so my wife scheduled an appointment with a technician at the local Apple retail store.

This was the first time I had been in an Apple store. The place was packed, but an employee approached me immediately and asked how she could help me. I mentioned that my wife had made an appointment. I was a few minutes early, so she asked that I make myself comfortable (there were lots of cool toys there to play with!), and a technician would approach me shortly. Right on time my technician, Sam, found me and asked how he could help.

I showed him the damaged iPad. He then referenced my home address and e-mail, and noted that I had never made a purchase directly from Apple. The next thing he said was: "How would you feel if Apple picked up the tab tonight and I sent you home with a brand new one?"

Just like that I was walking out of there with a brand new iPad! Remarkable when you consider the damage was clearly my fault and not warranted, and he knew that I was not a frequent shopper. I had never even made a purchase from an Apple retailer - EVER!

Clearly a moment of truth for Apple, and they aced the exam.

Here's what's interesting: The exact same thing happened to me. It wasn't a fluke. It was company policy.

Brilliance rarely happens by accident. It happens by design.

56. FIRST, DO NO HARM

Another old friend, Jennifer, told me a story that she's allowing us to share.

When I see your stuff about shareworthy service, I always want to comment about a shining star of service, technology and media - Cleveland Clinic.

I had some major health issues in 2008 and early 2009 and had the opportunity to visit their main Cleveland campus, and remain in contact with them since.

Service:

When you initially phone them, they ask, "Would you like to come in tomorrow?" I almost passed out! I was armed with my list of contacts, referral source, and list of validations for my visit.

I went there for one appointment with one doctor and department. He said, "I have some colleagues I'd like to have weigh in on this," and asked "How long can you stay in the area?" We were currently booked in for four days, but were flexible.

You might be thinking that I sat around in waiting rooms all day in the hospital. Nope. They simply asked me to stay within forty-five minutes of the campus. We went to Rock 'N Roll Hall of Fame, dinners out, shopping, etc. My cell would buzz. Next appointment: Bldg X, Room Y - 4:00.

The campus is clean, beautiful, lots of art & fountains ... and they have great sushi in one of their "store fronts" (no food court).

They have "Red Coats"- a small army of volunteers and paid employees, all easily identified by their red jackets. They are standing at all major hallway intersections and are happy to help you from point A to B, recommend an area restaurant, or anything else you need. Loved those folks!!!

The doctors see you on time, and they make sure you thoroughly understand the situation. It's like they seem to actually understand that you might be slightly whacked out at the situation and overwhelmed by the medical-eze.

You never see a "patient." No beds or wheel chairs with hospital gown clad people being wheeled from there to there. If the patient is able to walk from exam area to exam area they get re-dressed and do so. If they have to be transported they are taken through back halls rather than being paraded through common areas or waiting rooms. No clutching the gown shut in back – yikes!

Media:

Great website. Correction - AMAZING website with a plethora of info. Strong social media & interesting Facebook posts.

They create many videos for YouTube, their own site, etc.

Technology:

They have this great system called "My Chart," which allows the patient to manage health information and update their chart with new information, prescriptions, etc.

The fact that I could "enjoy" my time visiting a hospital during a very difficult situation sticks with me still today.

You take care, Jen. It was great to know you were in amazing hands.

57. IMPLEMENTING SHAREWORTHY SERVICE

I have been actively working on a theory for a couple months now, but I've been thinking about it for yeeeears. Two clients are beginning to test it. A couple more may follow.

As always, we will continue to increase our marketing budget as a percentage of sales, but we will be lowering our advertising budget.

Huh?

For years, owner-operated companies spent bazillions on things like the yellow pages - pouring buckets of cash into the last refuge for people who have no preference. Now, many of those same companies are using some of that money to buy bags of magic beans from social media experts.

Don't get me wrong. I think social media's a fantastic tool for listening and deepening a relationship and doing research and addressing customer concerns and sharing videos of singing dogs and stuff. It's just not a broadcast or direct response medium. For most owner-operated companies, social media's just terrible at direct response.

So my clients are participating in a grand and frightening experiment. We're going to begin taking part of our ad budget and putting it back into our company's best customers: our employees.

My partner Roy has said a million times: *You cannot improve what you do not measure and reward.*

Most managers love the measure part, but they turn the other way and whistle when you remind them about reward.

To implement this program, we started by asking these best customers - our employees - a series of questions about their ideal rewards, large and small. To get them to buy into this new way of thinking - that each employee is part of the marketing department - we had to start by painting a picture of what's in it for them. Each of them has a different carrot at the end of the stick. If I'm right - if we do our job correctly - we'll be able to reward them mightily.

How about you? Do you know what your team - your best customers - want, need and desire? I don't mean "more money." I mean specifics. Each one.

Does it bother you that you don't know?

Then, we have to ask them more questions. You have to ask them questions about what would cause a customer to *want* to share an experience with your company.

You have to ask them about professionalism and kindness. What the defining characteristics of each one looks and feels like to your customers. You have to ask them for specifics.

You have to pull out worksheets with the fourteen facets of shareworthy service and ask these most important customers of yours how each one could be dialed up with your company's customers. Ask for specifics. Ask each employee. First, ask them not to share answers so you can see individual results. Then do it again and collaborate on answers.

You need to ask your employees what YOU can do to deliver shareworthy service to them. After all, they are your best customers.

What do they need from you? What resources can you provide them to help them help your customers?

You're going to have to ask them.

Wait. Isn't this an awful lot of work?

Absolutely.

Then, how can you measure and reward these tactics? If you have a shareworthy service contest, what are the ground rules?

You know who needs to set them? Your best customers - your employees. They need to OWN IT. They are uniquely qualified to be specific about definitions, systems of measurement, rewards big and small, and implementation.

A funny thing's going to happen, I think, on the way to this new world. You're all going to have a heck of a lot of fun along the way. You're really, really going to enjoy coming to work every day sharing stories of your own.

We're going to continue advertising, don't get me wrong. We're just going to focus on media that allow us to harness the powers of emotion and story. And those stories aren't going to be about margin killing.

Groupon? Eat it, Groupon.

Customer service is the new accelerant. Most companies say they need a Facebook page. Why? I'm pretty sure they'd be better off focusing on delivering service worth sharing.

You want more likes?

Great. Give people something to actually, you know, like.

Of course, I could be wrong... about all of it. Are you ready to jump out on the skinny end of the branch and try it with us?

58. A LISTENING EXERCISE

The most common sales rep frustrations I hear from clients and small business owners across North America:

Sales reps don't listen. Sometimes they act like they listen, but I'm pretty sure they're just nodding and waiting for me to finish so they can start talking again.

Want to learn to actively listen?

It requires practice.

In your next sales training, pair up into twosomes.

Pick a conversational topic. It can be as simple as, "Tell me about your day yesterday," but it should be something that requires a bit of storytelling.

Sit in chairs facing one another. Person A will tell his story to person B.

They must maintain eye contact, and person B cannot interrupt. Understand that: Person B may not say anything. Person B's only job at this point is to listen.

Then, switch roles. Person A listens. Person B tells.

Once finished, go around the room with each Person B telling Person A's story and vice versa.

It's more fun if you have a colorful, emotional topic such as, "Tell me about your favorite family vacation," or "Tell me about your most embarrassing moment."

Do this once a week for the next twelve weeks. You will see dramatic improvements in connecting with not only clients and prospects, but also with friends and family, too.

59. SMOKING KILLS CURB APPEAL

I had just finished meeting with a client in Illinois when I headed to one of my favorite spots for lunch.

It has everything:

Great ambience? CHECK.

Great food? CHECK.

Planter by the front door filled with cigarette butts, empty packs and trash? CHECK.

It's a shame ... because all the great advertising in the world won't overcome me sharing that photo on Facebook.

My friend Darren replied, "If their planter looks like this, it's a good indication of what their kitchen looks like!"

Eww.

My business partner Mike Dandridge – an expert on how businesses improve customer experiences – taught me the term for this:

Micro-Associations

Consumers connect dots – even when no natural line exists. We invent them. Mike shared this quote from Donald Burr, former CEO of People Express Airlines:

In the airline industry, if passengers see coffee stains on the food tray, they assume the engine maintenance isn't done right. - May 5, 2002

It's true. Darren knew it. You know it. I know it.

But the good news is, it's so easy and inexpensive to fix. Just make sure you add it to the server or busser's list of side work.

Just please make sure he or she washes his hands before returning to work, okay?

Oh, and P.S. – If this were your client, would you tell them? Would you have the courage to speak up and tell them it was hurting the effectiveness of their advertising campaign? Help them connect the dots.

60. THE STICKY BUSINESS OF BBQ

One BBQ restaurant in my town caters for $7.50 a plate.

That includes two meats, three sides, and a bill.

You don't get plates or napkins or serving spoons.

Oh, and you're serving 3,000, or you're a regular customer and ask for a discount?

Sure thing. For you, it's only $7.50 a plate.

Another BBQ restaurant in my town caters for $8.95 a plate.

That includes two meats, three sides, utensils, napkins, plates, serving spoons, and moist towelettes.

It also gives the business owner flexibility and headroom (or margin) to make anyone he so chooses feel like they're getting a deal.

Whether it's a large order or a regular customer, business two builds in flexibility to ensure he can play favorites.

I'm not saying one strategy's better than the other, but one's probably a lot more fun.

The key is consciously choosing a policy and sticking to it.

61. THREE BEFORE ME

I saw a sign outside my client's office.

I loved it.

I didn't even know what it meant yet, but I loved it.

Outside Bonnie Young's office at Green Learning Academy in Calgary was a sign that read simply, "Three Before Me."

When I asked the director of the school what it meant, she said:

"Tim, remember here at Green Learning Academy, we strive to teach our children how to think, not what to think."

GLA's an amazing school founded on the principles of Don and Anne Green who were frustrated with the public education system's seemingly misplaced focus on rote memorization. The Greens' feared that we were raising a generation of robots - not independent thinkers.

There's the famous ad from Apple: "Here's to the Crazy Ones." That's Green Learning Academy.

About the sign, Bonnie said, "You know how easy it is for young children to come to you and want an answer? Well, here, before they can come to me with a question, they have to find three other places they could try to find the answer themselves."

"Maybe on Google, maybe in an encyclopedia, maybe a book or by discussing it with their classmates, but they have to try to first solve their own problem. The process matters usually more than the answer."

My business partner Roy gives equally good advice that's related and worth mentioning here:

"When you think you've found your solution (particularly on the internet), the home to information and misinformation alike, spend just another fifteen minutes trying to prove the answer wrong to ensure that what you've found was correct. Just another fifteen minutes should easily help you verify and confirm that what you found is true ... or untrue."

62. BUCK'S ICE CREAM AND MEAT LAB

Evocative names rock. Surprising combinations rock. Especially if they're not purely for show.

What's your hobby? Your passion?

Why not add it to your sign? BUT, be the first to do it. And be prepared - some will mock you. We call them the ankle-biters.

No, they don't put the meat in the ice cream, but on the campus of the University of Missouri you'll find Buck's Ice Cream and Meat Lab. The agriculture students run both operations for research and understanding. They take the dairy for the ice cream, and for the meat, they ... well, you get the idea.

I absolutely love this name. So do most people here in Columbia. One of the things we always do with visitors is head to Buck's for their famous Tiger Tracks ice cream.

People love the name. Sure, some make fun of the name. Sure they do.

Who cares?

Our brain loves surprise. We take delight from things we don't expect.

What's your passion?

I remember a man early in my career who performed alignments on vehicles. He also had a passion for marbles. Yes, marbles.

Terry's Alignment and Marbles could take care of all your alignment and marble needs in one fell swoop.

I remember Michael's Jewelry and Tanning Salon, Marilyn's Drive-thru Liquor Barn and Bait Shop (although come to think of it those two things are quite related).

Could you add something to your business name? Should you be Chapman Heating and Air Conditioning and Running Shoes? Or Michael's Sedation Dentistry and Magic Tricks?

How can you bring surprise and delight and be surrounded by your passions at the same time?

Why is it we all want to remembered but fear being laughed at?

Remember what David Freeman said in the quote at the beginning of this book about the goal of life.

Wear your passions proudly. Let 'em roar.

Who knows? You just may surprise a few people along the way.

63. WHERE THE OWNERS DROVE OFF THE ROAD

Like a lot of people, Billy and Brett dreamed of one day going from employees to owners.

It happened for them. After a lot of hard work and sleepless nights and huge risks, they went from selling cars to owning their own dealership.

They had big plans. They learned so much watching, you see, about what to do and, more importantly, what not to do.

They wanted to be involved in every decision. They wanted to celebrate the fact you could always ask for the owner and plead your case to him.

It was a radical approach for a major new car dealer.

You could always see the salesperson, or the salesperson's manager, or the finance manager, or the general sales manager, or the general manager, but the owner?

Are you kidding? Nobody gets to see the owner! We don't even know what he looks like!

Except my guys. The buck literally stopped with them.

What a dream it was to write ads for these guys.

As an ad writer, I can only use what you give me. The better the stuff - the more meaty the bits - the more powerful your message can be.

These guys were flying straight in the face of a long-held (and very frustrating for car shoppers) tradition of buck passing.

And it worked! Their business flourished. Their employees were happy. Customers were happy. The ad writer was happy.

This went on for over a year - the growth and success buoyed by a willingness to be accountable in an industry not, umm, exactly known for its integrity.

Stop me if you see what's coming.

They wanted to buy another dealership. They also wanted to go on vacation. And they didn't want to be there every day in every way anymore.

Which I can understand and so can you, but our meaty advertising strategy was about to go strictly vegan.

I wanted no part of it. It wasn't going to work. What had lifted their tide was about to sink back down into a swamp of mediocrity.

Now, they'd built equity in the market, so they'd still continue to be successful for a while, but things were about to change.

Billy and Brett started working with a different ad agency, and for reasons that surely must have been vanity, they switched from radio to television. Car dealers like television. Or, perhaps more correctly, car dealers like being on TV.

And the ads featured the nutty, wacky and zany Billy and Brett showing up all over town mugging for the camera, over-acting and *never telling us* who they were or why they were there.

But ... when you bought a car from them ... "you got them."

Whatever that meant.

Then they bought a billboard above the dealership. And put their heads on it. Nothing else. Just their heads and the logo.

Then they bought the other side of the billboard. And put the back of their heads.

And then we started seeing less and less of Billy and Brett.

They weren't involved in every deal anymore, and they didn't explain why it mattered that we got them when we bought a car. Heck, they didn't even tell us they were the owners of the dealership in their TV ads.

I suspect it's because they no longer wanted to be held accountable. And, I suspect they thought their new campaign worked for a while. I suspect it got great response from their friends, who said, "Hey, I saw ya on the TV there! That sure was funny!"

And then, they sold off most of their dealerships.

I like Billy and Brett. I always have.

I hope they go back to what got them that first dream.

64. A TALE OF TWO SALESPERSONS

This is a reminder to me: *Do not apologize for making a career out of advertising and marketing.*

If you take something away from it, too, then cool by me.

Salesperson #1's Tale

Salesperson #1 sent me four emails over two days urging me to buy something for one of my clients. Here's the last of the four emails:

I am fighting for page two ....have someone else starting to show interest, and I am crossing my fingers [your client] gets back with you (no, I am not a used car salesman, this is real).

Listen, I'm sorry, but it's kinda like you saying, "Well, I'm not racist, but ..." and then you proceed to render some horribly racist judgment.

If you have to say you're not a used car salesmen, I think you and I both know you're behaving like a used car salesmen. Right? Do you disagree?

Salesperson #2's Tale

Late last week, Salesperson #2 emailed me about a different client to let me know our annual contract (my clients typically all buy fifty-two-week contracts) was coming up for renewal in about a month and could we schedule a get-together to discuss renewal?

My client's business is weather-related, and our weather's been bad (and thus good for his business), so my client hasn't had the time to discuss advertising.

This morning, Salesperson #2 followed up to see if I'd spoken to my client yet. Nope, I said. Here's what she sent back followed by my reply.

Salesperson #2 wrote:

Sure, I understand. Thanks for getting back to me. I hope I didn't come across too much like a salesperson! Thanks again, have a great day.

Tim Miles replied:

You are a salesperson, though, and a good one! You're a great steward of your gifts and talent and your company, and you have no need to apologize for it!

People don't hate salespeople. They hate pushy jerkwad poopheads, and sometimes pushy jerkwad poopheads are salespeople, and sometimes they're kindergarten teachers, and sometimes they're carpenters.

Okay, they're not usually kindergarten teachers.

65. MY FAMILY'S THREE M'S

Like you, I suspect I'm a product of my raising.

My brother's the funny one. My sister's the creative one. My dad's the quiet, humble, polite, brilliant one. My mom is the incredibly-thoughtful, rock-solid, dependable, caring glue that holds everything and everyone together.

I was blessed to inherit or learn a bit of each. I'm kind of like the meatloaf of the family.

Now, not to go all Sesame Street on you, but the three great gifts the Miles family gave me all - fittingly - start with the letter M.

MEMORY

For reasons passing understanding, we can all remember the most minute of details about our family's events in the lives of others. While this makes for funny conversations around holiday tables, it's an extremely valuable tool when growing and fostering relationships.

Struggle with it? Make an effort.

Do your best to remember things about people. Remember their children's names. Remember birthdays. Notice when they get a haircut. Ask how their class is going.

These things matter.

The same is true of remembering the particular language of a particular kind of business. If you can speak to a business owner or a vendor in the language and vernacular of the business owner or vendor you have a greater degree of credibility.

(Please note this is the opposite of what you should do when writing copy. You should always talk to the customer in the language of the customer about what matters to the customer, right Roy?)

MANNERS

I suspect there's no greater gift ... and nothing brings me more joy ... than to watch my young children say "thank you," "yes please," "no thank you," "yes, sir," and "yes, ma'am."

Have you been to an airport lately? You can witness exactly who had parents raise them with manners and who did not. The seas part for those with manners, where a simple look of kindness and patience, a "thank you" or "take your time" moves mountains versus the whiny self-important jerk face who treats people rudely.

You learn so much about a person by how they treat others - most notably people who they perceive to be beneath them. The funny thing is that treating others with respect takes exactly the same amount of time as treating others badly. Why not simply choose the former versus the latter?

THE THIRD 'M'?

Monical's Pizza, of course.

66. SHAKESPEARE'S PIZZA'S SECRET INGREDIENT

"It's the pizza, stupid ... and maybe the beer."

So begins the mission statement for one of Columbia, Missouri's cultural icons: a self-proclaimed pizza dive known as Shakespeare's Pizza.

People come from wide and far and close and narrow to line up to eat their pizza. No pasta. No burgers. No fried ravioli or stuff. Just pizza and a few salads and both Coke AND Pepsi.

What's their secret? It probably won't come as any surprise they have several. Many of which have absolutely nothing to do with pizza.

Last night, they provided pizza for another client's neighborhood party. The client set up shop at a local park with games and music and a bounce house and other means of assorted funnery.

Two of Shake's Secrets: My client advertised that pizza would be served from 6:00 - 8:00 PM. Shakes started serving about fifteen minutes early and had the 200 ordered pizzas delivered in three flights rather than all at once.

That way, the pizza was always hot. If you were hungry ahead of the expected time (5:45 PM), you got a piping hot slice, but if you showed up at 7:30 PM, you didn't get a lukewarm, chewy, ninety-minute-old slice. Yours was just as piping, bub.

Sure, it takes a little extra effort. Build a little extra effort into the price. That piping hot pizza is marketing, friends. It's a language that communicates to guests that Shakes rocks, and it communicates that my client rocks, too.

Shakespeare's helped improve the event and continued to reinforce the positive image of the business.

My partner Roy recently told me that "advertising is a tax you pay for being unremarkable."

Often, the cheapest form of marketing is delivering a remarkable product or experience.

Why not look through your systems, policies and procedures and see where you can ratchet up the awesome?

"It's raising the anticipated price, stupid ... and maybe the beer."

67. THE TIME I FED THE TROLL

Every few weeks we get a nasty email about our advertising. This doesn't bother us as we understand that ads constructed to attract consumers should, by their very nature, also repel a few.

The ads you don't want to catch yourself writing are the ones that don't make anyone feel anything.

Last year, our ads made Lowell reach for his keyboard and head over to our Contact Us Form:

Your radio commercials that I hear on KPAM are juvenile. Please tell us what me might find on our roofs – not "yukkies and nasties." We're adults for crying out loud.

Now, I usually let it go. But he emailed a couple more times with equally negative spew. And, in a way I thought Lowell had a point in his first email that would make for a fun radio ad and also give him what he wanted.

You can hear it at: www.GoodCompanyStuff.com.

I loved it. Client loved it. The station reps loved it. The client's friends told the client how much they loved it.

We were getting tons of response.

Only problem was – we just weren't getting tons of results. Our number of generated leads fell off dramatically.

Whoops.

We pulled it off the air and learned a cautionary lesson or two about feeding trolls.

Stick to your plan. Remember – the people who leave angry-at-the-world comments on your local paper's website? It's the same seven people day after day.

Never confuse response with results.

Respect the Law of Attraction.

Don't feed the trolls.

68. HOW NOT TO EMAIL A BUSINESS OWNER

Hi Tim,

Remember me? I bonused [your client] some ads for Christmas? :)

There schedule ends in a few weeks, so I thought you would want to renew especially since the location [in city] is somewhat new. What are your plans for [client] for this year?

Maybe we could get together with a phone call?

Would you mind momentarily standing in for the rep whose email just arrived in my inbox?

I didn't ask for your bonus ads. You just told me you were going to do it out of the kindness of the station's heart. Guess not. Now, you're trying to use them against me? How many ways does that suck?

You used the wrong form of "there."

You're presumptuous without offering solutions.

My plans are none of your darned business. We've never met. In July, I bought a one-off schedule from the woman you replaced in December.

Two days ago, you left a message on my home phone letting me know you'd like to "get together to figure out how you can help me help your client."

I don't know. Maybe it's not that big of a deal. I think the punctuation-smiley-face-thing boiled me over.

But I don't email angry. In fact, I don't respond to an email like this via email. I'll either call or ignore you. I'm not sure yet.

But I had to type it out of my system. Thanks for letting me vent.

Yours in passive-aggressiveness,

Tim

69. A BETTER WAY TO EMAIL A BUSINESS OWNER

A colleague, journalist, and now ivory-towered academic asked how I might have written the salesperson's email in the previous chapter. He's the instructor-type, you know. And, as usual, Joey was right.

I sat down and – in about six minutes – wrote a draft and made one round of edits to this email.

I tried to compare apples to apples. I include a mention of bonus spots and one of those punctuation-smiley-face things that irritated me so much in her email.

Okay. Here's my attempt to write a better, more persuasive one. Remember the goal of both letters: To Get More of My Client's Money.

Hi Tim,

I'm [media rep] for [radio station]. We've never met but I replaced [previous media rep] at [radio station].

During the holidays, I left a message just giving you heads-up that your initial grand-opening flight for [client]'s location in [town] will expire at the end of January.

Time flies, doesn't it?

I see from her file that you already feel you have a strong strategy and she wrote that "he told me he'll be the easiest client in the world if you really just do what he asks and give him the lowest rates possible." :)

I would certainly like to try to keep your business with us. I can offer you some tremendous rates, and you already know we're a good fit geographically. I think I can bring [client] a lot of local people for the money.

Would you mind if I showed you what I have? I can send it via email, but I'd really prefer to meet you so I can look you in the eyes while I present, and we can both put faces with names.

You're in Columbia? I can come to Columbia on Monday, Tuesday, or Thursday next week, or I'd be more than happy to buy you and [client] lunch in [her city] anytime next week.

I talked to my boss, and we're going to extend your contract at no charge for another two weeks to give us a chance to talk if you like.

What do you say? May I buy you lunch, meet with you, or at the very least email you what I have to offer?

Thanks for your time, Tim. And thanks for your business these past six months. I promise I can be the easiest rep to work with in the world.

[New Rep]

P.S. — This was the number I had on file for you. Do you have a different number you prefer I call? Do you simply prefer email? Please let me know.

Well? How did I do? What would you have done differently?

70. ADVERTISING & THE PIT

Advertising only accelerates the inevitable.

Good advertising will make a good business more successful more quickly and more efficiently.

Good advertising will make a bad business go out of business faster.

If you're in between – languishing in the Pit of Mediocrity – you'll try advertising and it won't work very well (if at all, depending on a few factors) – at least, not nearly as well as it could.

There's a billboard for a convenience store I see every time I go to St. Louis that drives me bugnuts crazy:

It's meant to look like either a Twitter or Facebook status update. It reads:

Fastlane: For Fuel, Food & Fun!!

Why does it bother me so much?

Because it's false advertising.

I've been a couple times to investigate.

It's not fun.

I mean, at all. I know that may come as a shock.

It's got gas and beer and Funyuns and Combos and all that.

Just no fun.

But I'm not arguing they should change the billboard to match the experience.

Imagine if they changed the experience to match the billboard.

Have you ever ... ever ... walked out of a convenience store thinking, "Oh man, that was awesome!"

I see an opportunity. How about you?

What if this convenience store spent six months visiting amusement parks, carnivals, Vegas, Branson and a few other places that sell fun for a living? What if they took notes and figured out ways to provide a head-shakingly fun experience at a convenience store?

Free whoopee cushion with every full tank of ... wait for it ... GAS?

Spin the wheel of canned cheese?

A dunk tank filled with Red Bull?

Who can make these things happen?

Suddenly, you've got a c-store everyone's telling their friends about. Suddenly, you've got people lining up to not only fill up their tank but come inside for your high margin snacks and joy buzzers and stuff.

Suddenly my kids are begging to stop at FastLane in Warrenton on the way to Grandmom and Granddad's house. And my wife is telling her mom friends. And some goober's on the web blogging about their relentless capacity for fun.

Oh, people will come, Ray. People will most definitely come.

Because you're a convenience store.

And our experience at convenience stores across America* is drowning in mediocrity.

Advertising messages fail for two reasons:

1. Companies don't speak to consumers about things consumers care about in a language consumers understand.

2. Companies don't live up to the promises they make in their advertising.

FastLane passes number one with flying colors. We all need fuel, food and fun.

They fail miserably at number two.

The easy road is to change the ad.

The company on the road less traveled changes the company. And that will make all the difference.

*I say "across America" because if you're ever in Halifax, Nova Scotia, be sure to stop by Milne Court to see how you run a convenience store.

71. WRITE A LETTER

Why is it that when we write ads, we tend to lose our humanity? The most cordial and authentic of us shed that which makes us fine friends, and we become ogres and trolls for hire - blunt instruments of shill.

Unblunt yourself. The next time you feel your ad growing with the bloat of adspeak and unsubstantiated claims - stop.

Stop writing the ad. Instead - write a letter.

Write a letter (or email) to one specific person about whom you care deeply - could be any friend or relative - about the product or service. Persuade him or her to purchase.

You'll sound real. You'll sound confident, too, because you'll have had to do your research beforehand to prove yourself convincing.

Don't be afraid to rolling-start the letter by first writing about your personal life and where you've been and what you're doing to ease into the product/service recommendation.

Last year, I found myself stuck in such a situation for a client.

I wrote a letter to my father.

Then, I produced our most successful ad of last year.

Dear Reader,

I wish you the same success by writing to one person who matters to you - stripping away the fakery and sounding simply real and simply you.

It's why word-of-mouth works so well, and it's why your post-letter ads will do the same.

Warmly,

t

72. NO, SERIOUSLY. WRITE A LETTER.

Roy's company - Williams Marketing - did some research a couple years ago and found that the average person in America receives two hand-written, hand-addressed letters with first class stamps per year.

TWO!

What an opportunity. I believe in this age where it's never been easier faster to reach out to someone with a text, tweet or email, that you should do precisely the opposite.

Find some killer stationery. Texture's a language - and a sexy language to boot.

Write one letter a day. Heck, write two. They don't need to be long. They just need to be real.

People say direct mail's working less and less well by the second, and there's no denying that fact, but it's not the medium. It's just that there's very little direct about it anymore.

Reach out. Touch someone.

73. READ BETTER WRITERS

Go out and buy Willie Nelson's *Red Headed Stranger*. Without the benefit of a lyric or tab sheet, sit down with headphones and transcribe the words to each song.

Then do it again.

After doing it a third time, you'll start to feel in - your heart and fingers - the voice of one of America's great poets and storytellers. You cannot help but make Willie's voice your own.

Then pick someone else – an author – and do the same.

Echo. Mimic. Transcribe.

Have you seen the film *Finding Forrester*?

Sean Connery plays a reclusive writer who teaches his young charge to find his own voice by first channeling the voice of a better writer through the mechanics of muscle-memory, by typing the words of his teacher.

You can do the same. Put down the *Golf Digest*. Put down *HVACR Business*.

As you read, so shall you - right?

If you want to write the language that moves people, read the language that moves people. Buy a little notebook to jot down words and phrases that strike you. Be not afraid to use them in moderation to get you started. Some of my recent notations:

"vague seek shelter," "piper at the gates of logic," "beyond the bounds," "the tollbooth of reason," "an irresistible mystery," "reluctant," "feigning," "poignancy," "lumber," and "conscientious."

Will I use them in copy? Maybe. Maybe not. The point is that I took the time to recognize the phrases as compelling. Once you begin to do the same, you can find your own voice.

It's hard, don't forget.

Writing's really easy. Writing well's extremely hard, and it takes a lot of time and practice and effort and practice and thought and practice to find your own true voice.

And, then, it's not really yours at all. Something of a paradox, eh?

My voice includes Merle Haggard, Ernest Hemingway, my parents, my wife, my friends, Patty Griffin, John Steinbeck, Seamus Heaney, Kurt Vonnegut, David Foster Wallace, David Ives, David Mamet, David Ramsey, David Owen, David Byrne, David Feherty, David Seagle, Tom Stoppard, Jeff Tweedy, Aaron Sorkin, Townes Van Zandt, my cat, my son, John Prine, Ryan Adams, Mary Chapin Carpenter, Shawn Colvin, Paul Simon, Bob Dylan, Robert Frost, Roy Williams, Ryan Patrick, Dr. Seuss, e.e. cummings, and many, many thousands of others.

Open yourself up to great writers. Echo them. Dig inside their words and thoughts.

The next thing you know, they'll take your mistakes and your awkwardness and call it your style.

Homework?

Go buy *Consider the Lobster* by the late David Foster Wallace. Pick up a Patty Griffin's *Living with Ghosts*. Go buy *Poem a Day*.

Dig inside their thoughts and words to uncover your own voice.

74. NO GREATER GIFT –
UNDERSTANDING TIME & MONEY

Whoooooooooooooooooooooooooooosh.

We met in 1993. In 2000, I stood up at his wedding.

Before we could sit down again, life happened.

Sound familiar?

Nearly ten years, 250 miles and 3.3 kids later, he's here visiting.

When you get a bit older, time tugs a little harder in the war against money.

They're two sides of the same coin, you know?

Time and money.

Offer one, and people will give you the other.

As one increases, my partner Roy says, the other must surely decrease. That's valuable information to a strategist and ad writer. Consider:

Friends visit from out of town ... they give you the gifts of time and company. You owe them a return gift, not just for this visit, but for chapters written ... in the history of you.

Hard to do that ... with the teevee on ...

Aren't the best afternoons and evenings spent simply ... poured out through the shared lazy expectations of nothing more potent than the telling ... and re-telling ... of stories, laughs, and lies?

For reunion and communion, there's no greater gift. A vintage moment of lazy ... framed by a setting that could only be harvested by the hands of time?

Wine: The conduit to company.

The A-Frame at Les Bourgeois: The farm of familiarity. A short drive on I-70 to the Rocheport Exit 115, then meander north a minute or two.

There's re-connecting ... and there's re-connecting at the vineyard. They cost exactly the same. It's more a matter ... of value.

When given the choice? Take the A-Frame.

For reunion and communion, there's no greater gift.

I'll give you another little taste of valuable information in the next chapter.

75. SWEETER WORDS & SHARPER VERBS

In the last chapter, I shared a script I wrote that basically said:

Les Bourgeois is a *great* place to spend time with friends in a *fantastic* atmosphere! *Experience the Les Bourgeois experience* at a place that's second-to-none! For all your get-together needs, try us.

Only ... I didn't write that.

But I've read and heard the equivalent about a bazillion times.

Haven't you?

Yes, I actually heard "experience" used as both noun and verb in the same sentence.

Next time – want to help your message go down a little more smoothly? Help your audience savor your sweet somethings by using words that reinforce the mental pictures you're trying to paint.

Here's what Les Bourgeois said instead:

Aren't the best afternoons and evenings spent simply ... poured out through the shared lazy expectations of nothing more potent than the telling ... and re-telling ... of stories, laughs, and lies?

For reunion and communion, there's no greater gift. A vintage moment of lazy ... framed by a setting that could only be harvested by the hands of time?

In just two short grafs, how many words reinforce the idea of wine?

"poured"

"potent"

"communion"

"vintage"

"harvested"

All atypical choices – yet they not only fit contextually, they also help to reinforce that which we're promoting: the elevation of a shared experience through wine.

The next time you want to spice up your copy? Start with your verbs.

Can you replace a yawning verb - or three - with better, more relevant-yet-atypical choices that sharpen your sequence of mental images?

Next, look at your modifiers.

A few choice modifiers – vintage and potent – can go a long way. Most typical modifiers – great or fantastic – waste your audience's time because they've long since been watered down of any real meaning through overuse.

In fact, go through your piece of copy. Whack the dullard modifiers.

Read it again once whacked. Does it lack punch? Revisit the verbs. Insert some tasty ones.

You just breathed new life into your flat copy. Cheers.

76. TWO PROOFREADING TIPS

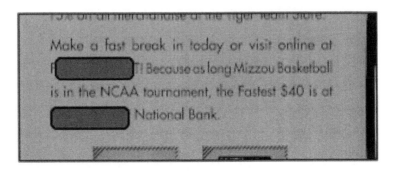

My wife got a very handsome direct mail piece from a local bank. It must've cost a fortune.

It had a typo.

Boy, have I been there. I've made that same mistake.

Here are a couple proofreading tips for you.

1.   Don't let the writer proof his or her own work.

Writers see things as they should be. Writers hear words they may have left off the page. Writers put proper pacing on perhaps awkwardly written lines.

A second person, and possibly third and fourth and fifth (particularly when tens of thousands of dollars are on the line), with no hint of the writer's melody, should be able to catch these things immediately without the burden of the writer's curse of knowledge.

2. Read the work aloud.

Our brains are way smarter than our mouths. Talk radio proves this every day. Our brains can fill in blanks and duct tape over mistakes. Our mouths don't do that. Our mouths will usually catch the mistakes and awkwardness.

First, read this sentence silently ... then read it again aloud:

Make a fast break in today or visit online at ourwebsite.com! Because as long Mizzou Basketball is in the NCAA tournament, the Fastest $40 is at Puckleschwartz National Bank.

Reading things aloud – and having others do the same – can easily help prevent mistakes and awkward sentences.

Take it from someone who's made dozens mistakes and written more than my fair share of awkward sentences.

:)

77. NOW, THAT SAID ...

This isn't sixth-grade English class.

Make up words. End sentences in prepositions. Do whatever you like.

Just make sure you know the rules you break and break them for a reason that helps.

I've written ads for sales so big the dictionary couldn't hope to contain them.

But I also have the *AP Style Guide* and everything *Grammar Girl* ever wrote on the bookshelf in my office.

I must say that what amateurs call a style is usually only the unavoidable awkwardness in first trying to make something that has not heretofore been made.
~ Ernest Hemingway

78. SHOW. DON'T TELL.

"Don't tell her you're courteous, son. Open her door."

In other words, don't tell her, son. Show her.

Welcome to the fertile fields of ad writing. I was cleaning up a presentation on ad writing that once provided a dozen meaty, actionable tips for making your ads more memorable. It's since grown to an eighteen pack, but in both presentations one of my big star performers is: Show. Don't tell.

Consider this radio ad I often use in my workshops and presentations:

$2,874.13.

Does that get your attention? Got mine. And it certainly got Jennifer's.

This is Francis Pass. Jennifer called us at Pass One Hour Heating and Air from over in Marion to schedule a repair on her air conditioner.

And our promise is: we're always on time, or you don't pay a dime. Sorry – reeeeally sorry – that in Jennifer's case we weren't on time. And she didn't pay 28,000 dimes.

Not gonna kid ya kid – it hurt. But, at Pass One Hour, respecting your time is simply the price of doing business … the right way. I think. Heck, what do I know?

I ate twenty-eight-hundred bucks trying to do the right thing. Maybe that's just goofy. But I just think – sometimes – doing the right thing … hurts a little bit.

Don't ya think? Jennifer does.

997-ssssssssssix-four-seventy-one. I'm Francis Pass, and I've got twenty-eight hundred extremely good reasons to make sure I'm at your house on time. Thanks for listening.

You can hear Francis' recording of this ad at www.GoodCompanyStuff.com.

Now, it's your turn. You've got great customer service? So what? Don't tell me you've got great customer service.

What, specifically, does the fact that your customer service is great do for me? How does it help me? What problems does it solve? How does it make me feel? Show me that. Show me what you've got.

What's the payoff? What's the result/benefit of using your product or service? Show me that. Dramatize that.

And get set to watch new customers open your door.

79. DRAMATIZING THE PROBLEM

"Would you believe," Brandon said, "that about forty percent of our business comes from wives who call because their husband and his three buddies tried to do it first and screwed it up?"

This was suddenly getting interesting.

Brandon owned an up-and-coming deck and fence treating company. He was talking about guys who were going to stain their own deck. Buy some beers, invite over some buddies ... how hard could it be, right?

This was a very profitable question for Brandon, and it got me thinking about dramatizing that problem by asking the question:

"Hmm ... what would an ad for that company - My Husband and His Three Drunk Buddies - sound like?"

A great copywriting technique is dramatizing an exaggeration of the problem, but when you do it, don't wink at the joke. Play it straight. That's where the humor gets its richness and makes its point so well.

I told Brandon that, in addition to our fee, I was going to need a thirty pack of beer. He, without question, said "no problem."

I liked Brandon right away.

That Friday night, fueled by Brandon's business expense, eight friends recorded the musical jingle and advertising campaign for My Husband and His Three Drunk Buddies in our home studio.

You can hear it at: www.GoodCompanyStuff.com.

It comprised forty-five seconds of a sixty-second ad. The rest we used to simply say what Brandon said - it's harder than you think. It's more expensive than you think.

Just let us do it.

But, if you want to try it first, let me know. I've got an ad campaign for you.

80. POWERWASHING STINKS LIKE ...

... dead August road skunk.

While we're talking about Brandon's company ...

I once read an interview with the sublime Mary Chapin Carpenter where she talked about the craft of songwriting. She paraphrased Bill Monroe when she said:

The songs are already floating out there ... lots of 'em ... all above you in the air. All you gotta do is reach up and grab one.

We're selling our home, and for the past three weeks we've been making it purty. I was assigned the task of powerwashing our fence by she-who-must-be-obeyed.

Powerwashing stinks, but I got an ad out of it. You can hear it at www.GoodCompanyStuff.com.

Ads live everywhere ... about the only rotten way to write one is to sit and stare at the blinking cursor.

Hacked-up drudgery comes generally from trying to make too many grand statements about someone or something.

We don't live our lives in grand statements.

Rather, we live even our peak moments through a series of little ones.

There's glory in the little moments – even the stinky ones (especially the stinky ones). Next time you have to write, reach up and grab one.

81. BEING THANKFUL FOR GROUNDHOG DAY

The Daily Tribune

GROUNDHOG DAY CANCELLED!

Lack of interest blamed on Chapman Family

Worry Over Six More Weeks of Winter Made Irrelevant by Chapman Heating & Cooling Offer

(COLUMBIA) - In a move that shocked residents in Central Missouri, the Chapman Family today lowered the price of membership into the Chapman Family Comfort Club through the end of February to only $123.00.

"It essentially removed the need for Groundhog Day," said Newton White-knuckle, mayor of Punxsutawney, "as now, with the Chapman Special offer, it really doesn't matter whether we have six more weeks of winter or six more weeks of spring - either way, families' homes will be perfectly and efficiently and, now, inexpensively finely-tuned in perfect comfort."

Groundhog Holds Press Conference; Announces Retirement; Will Learn Ballroom Dancing.

Why pick Christmas or Fourth of July?

Everybody else does.

Just like late-week broadcast schedules compete with the noise of all the car dealers and furniture stores doing SALE! SALE! SALE! ads, everyone seems to tie their events around the same holidays year after year.

Me? I like the wide open space of Groundhog Day.

Me? I like offering discounts to accountants and taxpayers alike on April 15th.

For me, nothing beats Opening Day of Major League Baseball or the first round of the NCAA Tournament.

At D. Rowe's, we've stocked up on Advil, Sudafed, tissues, cough syrup, meat, cheese, and all other items necessary for medicinal purposes and healing. (Pause) Just thought you should know ... in case you were planning on calling in sick during the upcoming basketball festivities. But remember - chicken soup is out. Smoked wings are in. Use as directed.

D. Rowe's - behind Walgreen's at the corner of Forum and Nifong. Four out of five doctors recommend us. Nobody likes that fifth guy, anyway.

Pick unusual holidays that arouse surprise and delight, but make sure you bridge between your event and the holiday. Make it odd and weird but still appropriate.

And one more - I almost hate sharing this one ... it's pretty valuable.

Why send Christmas Cards? Everyone sends Christmas Cards.

Beat the rush. Send a Thanksgiving card to your favorite/ best/regular customers. Include a gift card good anytime next year, plus a second for them to give to a friend.

And if you're a pizza place or you sell pinball machines or offer trips to Turks and Caicos, you're welcome to send one to me, too.

82. THE SHORT-SIGHTED RADIO SALES BUSINESS

I'm frustrated with radio.

Several of my clients successfully use radio, I know it works. I know how to make it work.

I think it's the service and training of those reps that makes me shake my head sadly.

Here's the story that started me typing:

My eye doctor's a kind man. I was one of his first patients shortly after he opened his practice and my wife and I moved to Columbia. That was 2003.

On the most recent visit, he said to me,

"Tim, you've been coming to see me for years. I know you're in the advertising business. I have eight or nine patients in the advertising business, and you're the only one who's never tried to sell me anything. You don't even like to talk about what you do. You'd rather talk about my kids and your kids how my practice is doing and other things."

"Mmm-hmm," I said, wittily.

He continued, "There's this one guy ... he's come into see me a couple times as a patient, but when he's here it's a pushy sales pitch about how I need his radio stations. He's evidently a director of sales or some big shot for one of the radio groups in town. He never asks me about my business. He doesn't know me, but he knows my practice needs to use his radio stations. And he's pushy about it.

"Finally, I told him, 'Listen, I was up twenty-eight percent last year, and I've grown every year I've been here ... without you.'"

I used to think radio's problem was too much rep turnover, and maybe that's endemic of a larger issue and problem:

Poor training, arrogance, impatience and an unwillingness to listen.

Hmm. Sad. Radio's been around too long to be acting like my two-year-old does sometimes.

One final thought ... my eye doctor asked me how much it would cost to hire me. The first thing out of my mouth was a number. I answered the question as asked before asking him why he wanted to ruin such a good thing. :)

Answering questions as asked ... hmm, maybe that's a good place to start the Radio Advertising Bureau's new training curriculum.

83. AD WRITING ADRENALINE

Painstaking research has taught me that staring at a blinking cursor for hours at a time gives you a headache, leaves you wanting to change professions, and makes you want to drink and/or cry.

Sometimes, you just need a start – a line or lines that may not even make the final but get your writer's blood flowing.

Here are three quick, simple tools I've used a million times to jumpstart my circulatory system:

1. Choose a Different Filter

The once-and-future Chris Maddock taught me this a few years back to not only get me unstuck but also to provide a different angle when necessary.

If John Cusack were writing your ad, how would it sound?

If William Faulkner were writing your ad, how would it sound? How about Ernest Hemingway?

What if that Randy guy from *American Idol* were writing? What about Ellen?

Pick a person or character with whom you're easily and accessibly familiar – write through his or her lens. Then, pick someone else.

Another way to think about this – say you're writing an ad for a car wash. Write the ad from the perspective of your car.

Give your script a different voice than your own. Once you fictionalize it, you tend to get out of its way.

2.   Write to the Rhythms

Throw on some headphones, put one musical track on repeat. Write to the mood and pace of the music.

Just start writing – get your left-brain out of the way. Let your fingers move with the music.

Keep doing it with the music on repeat for five minutes before really looking at what you wrote. I promise you there's at least one line on your page(s) that makes the final.

This works well when kinda-sorta marrying it with the first tip. First, try a piece of classical music, then jazz, then something hard and fast. Variation is the spice.

Need to write for a quiet place? Try something loud. Need to write an ad for a bangin' nightclub? Try something soft and smokey.

Those of you with access to broadcast production music libraries have it extra easy because you've get ready-access to volumes of instrumental tracks. Use them. You'll be done in no time.

3.   Just Pick One

Go upstairs real quick and pick a book at random off your shelf. I'll wait.

Okay, you happened to pick *The Curious Incident of the Dog in the Night-time*. Now turn to any page. You choose page 129.

Excellent. Now – go to the fourth paragraph and type the first line:

"I decided that I couldn't go home again."

No matter your client, couldn't that line open your ad? Just write around that opening line. Make it bridge to your benefit. Find your way home.

4. Just Say The Thing

If you're stuck … if you find yourself drowning in the sterile, homogenized "voice of business" and the sounds of ad speak, try this:

Write a draft of whatever it is you're trying to create that you know will totally and quickly be rejected because of its bluntness … but is still one hundred percent true.

Do you drink tap water?

Sure.

You're an idiot.

Wait. That doesn't go far enough …

You're a leg-humping, mouth-breathing, booger-eating idiot who must be too busy watching NASCAR to read the news.

Drinking bottled water?

You're a selfish, leg-humping, mouth-breathing, booger-eating idiot whose too busy filling landfills to care about your children's planet.

Using hard water for dishes and stuff?

You're a rich, selfish, leg-humping, mouth-breathing, booger-eating idiot who's too busy lighting your fat-bastard brand *cigars with $100 bills to notice you're ruining your appliances and plumbing.*

Rainsoft. Water systems for nice people on budgets.

If you're a jerk, call Culligan.

This is a great exercise for not-for-profit organizations - who can too easily get bogged down in trying to be all things to all people in the most amount of words possible.

Strip it all away. Just say the thing.

It's important to remember ...

Again, it's important to remember that what comes as a result of these jump-starts may or may not make the final. Each is only intended to jar your brain loose from its stasis.

Try them. They work. But, if rash develops, please discontinue use.

Oh, and P.S. – Good writing gets much easier when you commit – really commit – to good reading.

84. THE TIME SHERYL CROW WAS TONE DEAF

"They have their own voice talent for the ad," Aric said.

"Okay, anyone we know?" I asked.

"Sheryl Crow."

"Oh."

I was excited. I had written for national radio talk show hosts in both the U.S. and Canada, but this was different. I was writing for a world-class songwriter! Through a family member connection of the client, Crow was going to voice an ad for a local coffeehouse in St. Louis (Crow is from Missouri).

I was to write - a promotion for breast cancer awareness month (Crow is a survivor) - a sixty-second radio script for her to voice. I would write it, client would approve it and send it to her on tour. She would record it on her bus.

Naturally, this was my big break, right? I was going to dazzle her so brightly that she'd want me to help her co-write her next record.

Except it didn't work out that way.

Oh, I wrote my little fanny off.

I was there. (pause)

That's what you'll tell her. (pause)

On that day in the not-too-distant-future when doctors announce to the world they discovered the cure for breast cancer. (pause)

On that day, you'll remember how - in October of 2006 - you went to your local Kaldi's coffeehouse ... and helped change the world. (pause)

Hi. This is Sheryl Crow. One out of every eight women will be diagnosed with breast cancer during their lifetime. I know. I was one of them.

Which is why I've teamed up with Kaldi's Coffee Roasting Company to ask for your help and support in raising money during October - National Breast Cancer Awareness month.

Stop by a Kaldi's coffeehouse and look for my display. Proceeds throughout October will help us make ready for the day.

The day the world will cheer. The day families will embrace. The day we'll know we made a difference.

The day you'll tell your daughter, "I was there."

Rad, huh?

But it turned out Crow was tone-deaf to my copy.

It wasn't her fault.

She didn't know the melody - only the lyrics.

Had I provided her with a sample of how it sounded in my head, I would have had much greater success, and ... no doubt ... a publishing contract with her label.

Now, I always make an effort to let a client know how an ad sounds in my head before they ever read it.

There's always a voice, isn't there? Even when we read silently in the mind, we still hear someone's voice.

Here - listen to Crow, then listen to what I had heard Crow doing in my mind: www.GoodCompanyStuff.com.

Now, one other very important tip for writers that almost merits its own chapter: silence matters. Pauses are golden. If you overwrite, you rush your actor because broadcast ads are of a finite length. If it's emotional, underwrite. Give your talent room to play the melody.

85. BREAKINC NEWS: POLITICIAN FOR JOBS / ACAINST CRIME

You basically ignore yard signs, right? I mean, you may notice one after the initial plant, but then they all blend inexorably into the landscape until the sign gremlins come by in the dark of post-election night and take them down.

And then, you see one that aims to do a little more, and you get all excited until you actually read it.

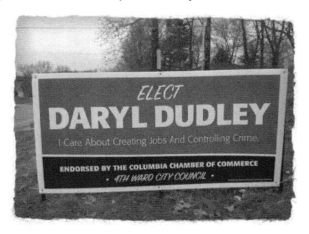

Oh, Daryl. I like you, man. You're a friendly cat who treats everyone with respect and even whimsy at the gas station you run.

I called your opposition and asked them if they were against more jobs and for more crime. They said, surprisingly, "Why, no. We're for more jobs and against crime, too."

In fact, when was the last time you met a politician who wasn't about creating jobs and controlling crime?

You threw another line on the sign, my good man. I applaud you for taking a chance to say something.

You just didn't say anything.

Those words blended into the political landscape a hundred years ago.

Sadly? Superficially? Even sprinkled with a little cheese? You know what could have helped you?

A line that simply said:

I'll do right by you.

No italics. No unnecessary quotes. Just that line.

When presented a choice with no real preference, we gravitate toward things familiar. By subconsciously introducing the mental image of the fine, upstanding Dudley Do-Right into their mind, you give yourself an edge when voters don't know any of you and they just feel obligated to pick someone.

But you wouldn't want to connect the dots for people with italics or those darned quotation marks. Don't wink at your own cleverness.

That's just one unsolicited idea, Mr. Dudley. If you win, you're going to get lots of them.

I'm excited you added another line. I'm going to vote for you. I just wish you would have done it right.

My partner Roy has often been known to say something akin to:

You don't define yourself by what you say you stand for. People define themselves to others by what they stand against.

So, Daryl? You want to get my attention and give me a glimpse into your world?

You want to cause me to act one way or the other? You can't be afraid of trolls, you understand.

Okay?

ELECT DARYL DUDLEY
I am against whiners and lazy people.

There. That's better. It does not solve the generality problem – I suspect most politicians when asked are against whiners and lazy people, but they just don't have the stones to say it out loud. They run the risk of ... gasp ... offending someone.

Guess what? In the words of Patricia Cabot, "you're not a hundred dollar bill ... not everyone is going to like you."

What do you think of Roy's theory? What are you against?

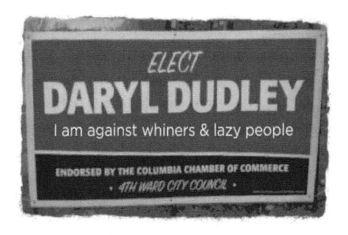

86. MY PERSONAL FAVORITE

People ask me all the time: "Of all the stuff you've done, what's your favorite campaign?"

It's a question that makes me uncomfortable a little because I don't like judging campaigns on any sort of artistic, subjective criteria.

Did it work? That's what I want to know. And how do you know it worked?

But I'll play along - with myself - and answer the question. Frankly, I'm not even sure the entire campaign ever ran, but it was for a clinic in Brisbane, Australia.

My friend (sorry, "mate") and partner, Craig Arthur, had asked me to come up with some concepts and copy for a series of cards. I won't go specifically into the strategy in case he wants to use it (or I want to use it here in the States), but it was brilliant. It's not what you think simply by looking at these cards.

Anyway, Craig asked me to pay tribute to lives well lived. I did it by looking through conceptual stock photography and using my imagination to come up with stories that correspond to the pictures.

It was just ... so ... much ... fun. And I think the stories are small (that's a compliment) and rich and true ... and they bridge back to the client. I, along with our partner Sonya Winterbotham, could have written a million of these.

Ignore the logo placement ... I just threw on a lo-res image. These weren't the finished products - they were simply comps.

See the campaign at www.GoodCompanyStuff.com.

It's another great tip for brainstorming, isn't it? Simply going to a stock photo site (or even just a search engine) and typing in some conceptual term.

Let your mind wander. Follow it wherever it leads. The results may rise up to surprise you.

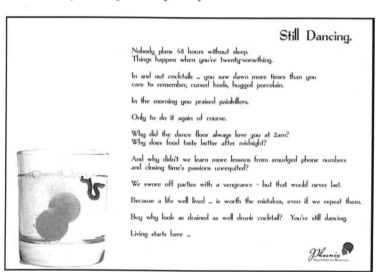

Still Dancing.

Nobody plans 48 hours without sleep.
Things happen when you're twenty-something.

In and out cocktails ... you saw dawn more times than you care to remember, cursed heels, hugged porcelain.

In the morning you praised painkillers.

Only to do it again of course.

Why did the dance floor always love you at 2am?
Why does food taste better after midnight?

And why didn't we learn more lessons from smudged phone numbers and closing time's passions unrequited?

We swore off parties with a vengeance - but that would never last.

Because a life well lived ... is worth the mistakes, even if we repeat them.

Buy why look as drained as well drunk cocktail? You're still dancing.

Living starts here ...

Phoenix
Rejuvenation Medicine

87. HOLIDAY ADS

"Should we do a Christmas greeting?"

I think most businesses go through this at some point or another (and heck, let's not even get started on whether or not you dare actually say "Christmas" or "Hanukkah" or give someone even the slightest hint of your personal beliefs.)

This isn't about that. It's about bad, generic advertising.

Most holiday greetings are a waste of time.

Most holiday greetings are interchangeable.

Most holiday greetings sound like the business ripped one of the Christmas cards down of the fireplace mantle and read it straight through - pausing only long enough to insert their own name a couple times.

Do you have a story worth telling?

Do you have something to say?

Then, yes, say it.

Francis did.

Hear his message at: www.GoodCompanyStuff.com.

So, yes, if you have a story with telling, if you have something to say, then yes, say it.

88. I'VE BEEN THINKING ABOUT YOUR WEBSITE

I've traveled all over giving talks and workshops. Something I try to do when time permits is offer up spontaneous website critiques for business owners and not-for-profit agencies in attendance.

Want to know a secret: It makes me look really smart, but it's really cheating.

People make pretty much the same ten mistakes over and over again.

Those ten mistakes are a different story for a different day.

But let me get you started.

Why do you have a website?

Seriously - what did you build it to help you do? Write it down. I'm not kidding. Ask your employees to do the same? Say it simply and plainly.

If your website is like any other employee (and, really, it should be thought of that way), do you have a job description and standards of performance for it?

Why not?

And do you measure anything? Do you even know what the heck "hits" means?

You cannot improve what you do not measure and reward.

Furthermore, are you a part of the web conversation? While you may have others build it, are you personally involved with its construction?

Wait - what do you mean it's already been built? A website's never done. Just like your home, you should be cleaning and maintaining and re-decorating seasonally and putting fresh, tasteful touches here and there.

And every once in a while, you need a major remodeling project.

Oops. I think I just switched metaphors. My bad.

Let me give you one last piece of advice in plain, simple, metaphor-free English, okay?

Ask the people who answer your phones regularly:

"What are the four or five questions you get asked by customers over and over again?"

Have them keep a sheet by their desk to jot down additional questions they might not think of right away.

Then, do the same with your retail sales people, or your outside sales staff, or your technical staff - anyone who regularly comes into contact with customers.

You need to make sure those questions and answers to those questions - in language people actually use - are easy to find either on your homepage or linked to from your homepage.

That should get you started. Call me when it's time for your site's ninety day review.

89. YOUR SPHERE OF CREDIBILITY

"What about a blog, Tim? Do we need a blog?"

Maybe. Do you like to tell stories? Do you like talking about the things you do?

Google and search engines love fresh, regularly updated sites stuffed with relevant content. You've got credibility, right? There are few better, less expensive places to demonstrate that credibility than on your blog and website.

That's a start. You don't even need to type them out. There's a great company out there my partners started, Shortcut Blogging, that does all the heavy lifting for you. You just need to be yourself.

But what the heck do you talk about?

Well ... if you strictly talk about your business category, you'll quickly not only exhaust your material but also bore the tears out of and repel those you wish to attract.

Thing is - you can obviously talk about anything, but some choices are better than others.

I call it your *Sphere of Credibility*. I capitalize it to make it sound important. I made it up one day when I needed something to call it for a talk I was giving.

I got the idea from a guy much smarter than me.

In 1959, Theodore Leavitt introduced the idea of a better business reality at Harvard Business School.

Leavitt said essentially that, for example, a mattress store wasn't in the mattress business, but rather the better reality was that they were in the business of providing customers a better night's sleep and more energy during the day.

Thus, a tire store didn't sell tires. They sold safety. Remember the Michelin ad with baby surrounded by the tire? That's a perfect example of what Leavitt understood.

Your sphere of credibility is similar.

If you're a heating and air conditioning company, you'll bore the pants off people talking about A Coils and compressors, but ... you can find ways to talk about the better reality of your business: providing comfort in the home.

But wait - there's more. A reader will give you the benefit of the doubt to talk with credibility and authority about comfort in general. If you shared a link, for example, about mattresses that'd be interesting to me.

Or vacation spots. Or comfort foods.

No, they're not HVAC-related, but who cares?!?

Continue to do this - share interesting stuff within your sphere of credibility, and you'll slowly and steadily build a strong association between your business and your larger reality.

I swear it's true. I've seen it happen time and again. I'm not making this up.

(Now, if I could just figure out a way to get vintage arcade games inside my sphere. If you have any suggestions, I'd be grateful.)

90. "WHO DO YOU WRITE YOUR BLOG FOR?"

I realize I guess I was supposed to say, "For whom do you write?"

Does that sound dumb and kinda 18th century to anyone else? Okay. Good.

I thought I'd share some insights into my workflow and motivation, and secrets to delivering (hopefully) quality content day after day on my blog.

Things started improving immediately when I wrapped my head around one truism:

Try writing to everyone, and you end up writing to no one.

Here's what I mean by that: Worrying about offending or being too specific or being too boring to the masses is a sure-fire ticket to, at worst, paralysis, at best, flaccid writing.

I write first for myself.

- Is this something I'd want to read?
- Does it feel honest?
- Unpretentious? Human?

Yes?

Then it's onto the second audience.

Depending on the post, I'm writing for ONLY one of four people.

If it's about customer service, it's an employee at a local company I've known for a few years. She's trying to do the right thing but often has to swim upstream.

If it's about strategy and advertising, it's a particular small business owner who's got more promise in her pinky finger than I had – at her age – in my whole body. She's going to take over the world. She just doesn't know it yet. I'm trying to keep her pointed in the right direction.

If it's about motivation and productivity, it's for a director of a small not-for-profit I know who we desperately need to stay enthused and keep fighting the good fight.

Finally, if it's about autism and my son, it's for my mom.

I really, truly don't write for anyone else. If you like what you read, awesome! Come along for the ride.

Choosing one person – imagining this one person reading ... being helped ... by the odd little thoughts in my head has helped make this big ole' goofy world a little smaller and a little more meaningful and a lot more consistent.

You should try it. Whether you're writing an advertisement or a proposal or teaching or delivering a sermon, try speaking or writing to just one person.

You'll quickly learn, as I have this past month, that we are more alike than we are different.

Like, for example, most of us don't care if someone ends a sentence with a preposition.

Sometimes, we all just need to be reminded, and that's what I'm here for.

91. PRACTICALLY SOCIAL

Blogs and tweets do not require salve – they require a little working knowledge and (very) little money. This multi-media presentation will give your audience a fun introduction and practical applications of new media such as blogs, websites, email marketing, Facebook, Twitter, and more.

It's here, it's unavoidable, and it can help any business willing to invest more time than money, but it's not a quick fix or magic bullet.

But, it's also not that complicated. The times are, indeed, changing.

Sure, life used to be simpler.

It seems like five minutes ago you could turn on your radio or switch between your three television stations and be perfectly content!

You could walk out to your mailbox and get your handful of daily mail. The only SPAM we knew came in a spiffy little tin.

Unsure who to call? Grab the yellow pages.

Then stuff started going off the rails, huh?

And now, day after day, we wake up with more choices, more options, more channels and more noise.

Things are busier, sure, but are they better?

Sorry to say I'm not sure that's the right question.

I'm not sure it's helpful, or particularly relevant, to bury your head in the sand, mumble about the past and long for simpler, sweeter times.

Perhaps it's best instead, don't you think, to rise up into the *Finding Nemo*-esque slipstream and ride the current into the future?

Want some good news? It's never been simpler.

There's never been a better time for you to transform your company's communications plan and marketing budget.

Want some better news? If you're good - really good - at what you do, and you like talking about what you do and how you can help people, there's never been a more financially efficient time in history to gain market share since the early days of the water treatment industry.

So, let's recap: A number of companies are poised to grab market share in the coming months without necessarily infusing their marketing budgets with hugs wads of cash. But, each of these companies has a rather similar set of defining characteristics:

1. They're very good at what they do.

2. They like talking about what they do.

3. They don't use economic uncertainty and consumer credit instability as excuses to pull an Eeyore and go all woe-is-me.

4. They're not trying to drive using the rearview mirror. They're looking ahead with eyes wide open.

5. They have a plan.

That last one's important.

One of the natural side effects of our recent explosion in technology is the sheer heft of voices and choices hurtling toward us. In 2007, the last time market research firm Yankelovich did such an estimate, a person living in a city saw perhaps as many as 5,000 messages a day.

How can you plan to rise above the noise?

Let me give you three ways that I learned them from an eccentric futurist who, it should be noted, is probably a wackjob. Just so you know. But stick with me.

Frequency

Imagine a woman calling you - madder than heck - and accusing you of false advertising. Then, you come to find out, she only uses your product every other week, but expects the results to be delivered all the time.

She isn't using as directed, is she?

Whatever tools and tactics you choose to include in your marketing plan (and that's really a different topic for a different day), you should plan to deliver your message to consumers for only as long as you plan to be in business.

Customers, and potential customers, have this annoying habit of caring about things important to them rather than what we think they think should be important. We're all too busy. We're all too alternately focused and distracted. We're all too over-communicated, unless you tell us and then keep on telling us.

When you understand that you need to be there - in their world - a little bit each week for the rest of your business' life, you begin to understand the degree to which you must scale your commitment.

Whatever your medium, whatever your message, use as directed.

Consistency

Do your messages – again, regardless of medium - have the same look, say and feel?

We're talking about word choice, pacing, white space, fonts, music and audio signatures, and so on.

Though every President or Prime Minister has a team of speechwriters, their mission is singular: to write in the distinctive voice of the leader. The same should be true for all your messaging.

Do they contain certain repetitious elements that allow these super-busy, back-button, over-communicated consumers to easily connect the dots from one of your messages to the next?

At our little ad firm, we first help our clients consciously develop style guides that assemble the defining characteristics of a message plan.

Your elements should fit your business naturally and authentically so there's no disconnect when a consumer chooses to do business with you, and they, too, should be with you for as long as you plan to be in business.

Relevance

Most critically - given our time and attention poverty - are you talking to consumers about what matters to consumers in a language that consumers understand?

Time and again, I've seen business owners who try and convince me that if the consumer only understood the nuance and intricacies of what they were selling, they'd for sure do business with them every time.

But consumers don't want to understand. As I said before, consumers have this nagging habit of caring about their own lives, their own worlds.

You're the invader here. You're the interrupter. You'd better darn well make it relevant to me, and you'd better do it quickly.

This is easier than you might suspect. Ask them. Ask your customers. In his magnificent book on customer service, *Customers for Life*, automotive legend Carl Sewell said that - probably like you, he "knew that intuitively, but I wasn't sure why. So we started asking customers what they didn't like about doing business with us, and they told us, quite often without mincing words."

Sewell knew, and deep down you know, too: "I started thinking about our company from the customers' point of view."

Armed with these three weapons, you can move forward fiercely into this undiscovered country.

Oh, and the wackjob futurist? Get this: some eccentric scientist evidently rubbed meat paste onto the tongue of a dog over and over again. Every time he did it, he rang a bell. Over and over - meat paste, bell, meat paste, bell, meat paste, bell. Word on the street is that suddenly this dog started drooling when he heard the bell.

And for his little experiment in frequency, consistency and relevance, they gave Ivan Pavlov the Nobel Prize for his study of conditioned response ... in 1904.

Ah, the good ole' days.

92. WHAT'S THE BEST WAY TO TRIGGER SOCIAL MEDIA?

Deliver an experience worth talking about.

93. MY FRIENDS LIKE THESE

There's never been a better (or more profitable) time to excel at delighting customers.

The thing is – it's pretty darned easy for every one of us to come up with a story about horrendous customer service.

What about good ones? Inspiring ones?

Who are the companies that deliver?

Let's take a look at the defining characteristics of legendary customer service and why it's never been more important (or more profitable) to deliver it.

In case you hadn't noticed, the Internet changed some stuff.

Now, in addition to being able to watch clips from Battle of the Network Stars, you can also spread the word about anything to dozens, hundreds, even thousands of friends (and they to theirs) with a few taps, points and clicks.

That's great news if you're extraordinary. That's really awful news if you're a boogerface.

To start my research into legendary customer service, I did what all astute professional scholars do: I went to Facebook.

Here's what a few Facebook friends had to say when asked what companies came to mind when thinking about legendary customer service:

Suzanne – Nordstrom. Never a hassle on a return.

Amy S. – Gates Barbecue. "Himayihepyou?" Always with a smile.

Amy M. – I appreciate never waiting in line at Target stores.

Melissa – Zappos. I know it's cliché, but it's true.

Joey – Here's a few that come to mind: Zappos.com — Unhurried, knowledgeable phone suggestions. Surprised to discover free upgrade to next day delivery when the shoes arrived. Southwest Airlines — I showed up a day early for a flight. No hassle. They fixed it, no charge. My local pharmacy (Logan Professional) anticipated my benefits year and ordered refills for me a few days early so the deductible wouldn't kick in. Ritz Carlton Battery Park NYC — usually out of my price range but I got a deal. Employees know your name by the second time they see you. Concierge went way beyond expectations.

Mike – Southwest Airlines for sure! Their customer service makes them the only ones I want to fly.

Renee – Amex. Had my card # stolen a month ago. No hassles, sure, but they handle everything so quickly. Love them!

Kristi – HyVee has a "no point" policy that their clerks are supposed to follow. They are to walk you to the thing you're looking for instead of just saying or "pointing" to the general direction where the product it located. In my experience, my HyVee has followed this policy every time.

Kristi (Part Deux) – When it comes to a phone or internet order, the company Plow and Hearth provides hands-on experience for all of their operators with the products they sell. When I called to ask questions about some curtains I wanted, the operator went on and on about the curtains because they were new to the catalog and they had had a training session the week before on all the aspects of the new curtain. I was awed b/c I was dealing with someone who knew the product and wasn't just reading info off a screen! When I asked if that was common, she said all the operators were required to have had some kind of hands on experience with all the products–wow!

Kyle – If you want to go with a local company/business, I'm really happy with Landmark Bank. They have always been super helpful to me when I have questions about my money.

Megan – Ditto on Zappos. And locally, Lone Star is actually pretty amazing. I think it's important to remember the small things – they always ask me to cut into my steak to make sure it's cooked right so they can immediately take it back if it's not. This doesn't happen at other places and it drives me bonkers because I always have to send it back!

Lori – St. Louis Bread Company. They gave my friend the wrong order in the drive-thru. She got home and called them...they brought the correct order to her house and gave her free dessert and bread!

Nanci – The Learning and Performance Support (LAPS) Team at MUs College of Ed ROCK! They keep all stakeholders in the College of Ed working and up-to-date on leveraging technology... I couldn't do what I do without them...and I not only say thank you in person, I write letters with specific actions they take to support my work and send them to the DEAN....

Bret – Chick-fil-a is one of the best. Go to any store and say "thank you" and they will never say "you're welcome."

They will always say "My pleasure". Best fast food service ever.

Bethany – Kohl's has an excellent return policy. No questions asked. For someone who often misplaces receipts, I appreciate that. Plus, they have a Kohl's Care Team that volunteers in the community.

Jess – One of my dear friends was diagnosed with breast cancer so she and her fiancée moved up their wedding by nine months, and we all pitched in to plan their wedding in two weeks time. When the shop where her dress was ordered told her that her dress was in Springfield, she told them her story and the store manager drove in her car three hours each way to get it to her.

Kelly – Have you seen the info about Pike Place Fish Market in Seattle? They have a strong work ethic when it comes to customer service. I saw a video a few years ago that they put out about how they improved customer service. Hope this helps :)

How you about? Who do you think is shareworthy?

There's never been a better, or again, more profitable time to excel at delighting customers.

Oddly enough, it's also never been simpler.

The question on my mind is this, though: Just because it's simple … is it easy?

94. MY SOCIAL MEDIA ADVICE TO HEIDI

At the risk of ticking off about a bazillion social media experts, I can tell you - for free - how to begin a social media program for your owner-operated company.

Blog, plus pick one. Pick Facebook, for example.

Then, maybe once a day, share a story from inside your sphere of credibility. A link to someone else's content.

You won't pick up many fans of your page. Get over it. It's a marathon, not a sprint, but if you share stuff that interests people, you will slowly build an audience.

The same is true of your blog.

Interestingly, search engines will reward your efforts, too, but not overnight.

Don't give up. Keep at it.

Make sure you listen. Use search engines and social media to listen way more than you talk. Find conversations and share without selling. Provide more information than anyone else.

That's it.

If you're not in an inherently social business category - if you're not a restaurant or bar or amusement park - don't expect too much too fast.

In fact, don't expect much at all. That'll help. Lower your expectations and be wary of anyone who tries to sell you a bag of magic social media beans.

But you can do it, and do it well, and there's little cost, except your time.

95. SIX SOCIAL MEDIA TIPS FOR SMALL BUSINESS

I recently sat through a presentation on social media put on by a local community magazine. Many towns have them. They feature articles about, coincidentally, sponsors and do "Best of" polls and have a few pages in the back of beautiful photos of beautiful people attending beautiful events.

The presentation left me troubled that social media was just too vast to grasp for a fifty-something small business owner.

So, I went to my own Wizard. My friend and partner (and world-renowned marketing speaker), Bryan Eisenberg. He consults the Dells and the Universal Studios and the Volvo Internationals of the world.

Recently, he delivered a keynote to a small business expo in Connecticut and shared with me the six basic tips that he gave to them.

Here's Bryan:

Step Number One: You have to stake your claim.

A few years ago it was Myspace that was hot, now it's Facebook, now it's this one ... social media networks are coming out left and right, and we don't know what the next strong one is that's going to hit. Right now, Four Squares is looking pretty good, not positive, but it's worth at least owning your brands on each of these.

So I recommended a site called <u>www.knowem.com</u>. You can go there and it will give you little links and check the availability for your name. Don't do it yourself. It will take you forever. For like twenty or thirty bucks they'll actually go and register all the available ones for you.

So just stake your claim, own the position. The thing about it is early real estate. The same way I bought each of my kids a domain name when they were born, it's like real estate because you don't know what neighborhood is going to get hot later.

Make sure that you stake your claim on Google Local Business Center for their local advertising because that's going to be a major play with mobile phones, and everyone is moving to Smartphones, iPhones, the Android devices. What they're doing on local advertising is going to be mind blowing, so you want to be sure that you have the ability to do everything you can there. So run a search on Google for Local Business Center. And then of course, same thing with sites like Yelp. Make sure you claim your business there. It's really important to do that.

Step Number Two: Become a good listener.

I have somewhat of a religious background. I'm not a very religious person, but one of the early lessons I learned from a very intelligent Rabbi that said, "Look, you have one mouth but two ears, use them in those proportion." So listen twice as much as you speak and that really is what social media is very good at doing.

So, do a search on Twitter or use tools like TweetDeck or HootSuite to set up some of these searches and do the searches for your brand. Do the searches for your category.

So you can type in something like "hotel" near a particular zip code within one hundred miles. I showed an example of how I was in Stanford, Connecticut, and I searched hotels within one hundred miles of its zip code, and one of the first tweets was someone asking, "Hey, I wonder if the Ace Hotel has a quiet public spot." Now if I were the Ace Hotel and I saw that, I'd be the first one to respond to this person saying "Hey, my name is June. When you come into the hotel look for me, and I'll make sure you have a quiet spot to do whatever you need for that hour."

Great listening to drive your brand. That's what makes you remarkable.

Step Number Three: **Use social media to show off your expertise.**

What social media allows you to do is not think of yourself as a retailer or a manufacturer. Today, people need to think of themselves as publishers, because everybody is a publisher. If you have a camera phone, if you can go on Twitter, everybody can publish to that. You can publish a review - everybody is a publisher. You need to start thinking of yourself and your business as a publisher and use it to show off your expertise: why you develop products a certain way, why you choose the inventory you choose, why your buyers are so spectacular, how to take great care of your lawns, how to make sure your pipes don't freeze this winter, how to easily take care of yourself - show off your expertise.

Step Number Four: **Use the platforms to show off your value as well.**

Leverage what other people talk about. Share it with others.

One of my favorites is Paul Stoltzfus from Wise Grass. I love Paul. I remember the first time he was in a class I taught, and we actually worked together and came up with the name Wise Grass (he does landscaping in the Lancaster area). One of my favorite things about his website is that you can click on "Visit

A Show Lawn Today," and he linked together a Google Map and created what's called a mash-u. This is part of Web 2.0 social media technology. He has his own little database, and you can actually see little pins and you can visit with the Google satellite view the locations of where he's done his work. So you don't need to take his word for it, he can show off his great work by leveraging the technology that social media has available. Incredibly, incredibly powerful.

Step Number Five: Develop a following – tell people where you are.

One of my favorite examples is the Kogi BBQ on Twitter. Kobe BBQ is a van that sells Korean Barbeque in Los Angeles. How many followers do you think a typical food van might have? Last time I looked they had 52,660 followers.

Their food is obviously pretty remarkable. But what's remarkable about them is that they tweet where their van is going to be. What about if you're the local restaurant and you tweet "Hey, special today only for my Twitter followers. X will not be on the menu. Come in and order it. " Or "Here are the soups of the day. Call us for your delivery." So many ways to do this and let people know where they can follow you. Give them your Twitter address. Put it on a card or have a screen right there where they can just click a button and follow you. Whatever you can do to make it easy for potential customers.

Step Number Six: Use what people are already doing and leverage their activities. *I think this is the most important step.*

One of the examples, and I mentioned this one to you earlier, is something like Foursquare. Foursquare is a location-based service. What that means is that you're on your cell phone and the GPS on the cell phone says "Hey, I'm at Gold's Gym on

King's Highway." So you have to check in when you're in that location.

As a great example, I show this one little café that says "Okay, if you're the mayor, (which means you've checked in a certain number of times) your drinks are free today." So imagine doing that and say you know what, if I'm the Gold Gym's owner, I get to say, "If you're the mayor, free smoothie today, free spin class," or if I'm the jewelry shop, "Free something," whatever it is you have the opportunity to leverage it.

One of the other great examples I share with people is something that IKEA did but that everybody can do. You come out with new merchandise, ask people to come in and size it for you and take the pictures so you can put it up on Facebook. Take all your new fashions, because what IKEA did is they took pictures of their showrooms and let people tag their favorite products and they used the photo tagging feature readily built into Facebook to promote the items in the store because they wanted those items so much, and they got a chance to win those items. Leverage what people are doing, watch other people's activity and do it. And then, most importantly the way you're going to become successful, be remarkable.

That's the number one secret. Today it's easier for the customers to tell people how remarkable you are. You don't have to wait for the slow pace of word of mouth.

It's overwhelming that the number of social media platforms are in the tens of thousands today. But there are a few places I would focus on, and again, they're where most of the traffic is. You want to go where your customers are. It may be a local community center that has a whole area, you want to be involved there. You want to be a member of your community. If your community is on Twitter, be there. If your community is on Facebook, be there. I'm pretty sure you can do better on Facebook, because Facebook has more members than the whole

United States has population today. If Facebook was a country it would be the third largest country in the world. One hundred million people log into Facebook daily, everybody is there, so you have to be there. If everybody starts moving toward Four Square then be there, if everybody starts going to Joe Schmo's Together Place, be there. But most importantly, just be remarkable.

I just want people to get this and not be scared of what's going on. Technology can be daunting, but the fundamental root of all this: it's all fundamentals of business and communication, it just evolves a little bit, that's it.

My sincere thanks to Bryan for enlightening me, and hopefully, you too. Maybe you now have a glimpse into why companies like Google, Forbes and HP call him to speak to their audiences.

BEING

96. ARE YOU CONTRIBUTING TO MORE THAN YOUR OWN SELF-INTEREST?

Since our son was diagnosed with autism, I've been blessed to speak to more than a thousand not-for-profit organizations. My message is essentially:

For now, at least in western society, greedy is no longer goody. (Sorry, Gordon.)

In this interconnected world where the emerging generation longs to marshal their forces towards some greater collective good, and where aging boomers look for something new to occupy their time that makes them feel like they're making a difference, your company needs to look and work and make sure that you're supporting more than your own self-interesting bottom line.

What is your company doing to give back what?

Today's emerging generation is looking to see not only what you say but what you do?

They want to make sure that you share their values and interests in trying to make the world or your community a better place.

Don't know where to start? Ask your children. Ask your employees. Develop a program that measures and rewards the best places to commit and make a difference.

Because of the way the world has shifted, Western society has swung from an inward focused, me-generation to an outward focused, we-generation.

In our lifetime there has never been a better time to do good works.

This may run contrary to what you would think given the state of our economy the past couple of years, but you would be mistaken.

However, there is a second corollary that needs to be taken into consideration. While there has never been a better time to do what it is you do, there has also never been a more important time for you to be *good* at what you do.

Troubling times are like a forest fire. They thin the herd - the herd in this case being the disinterested, same-as-it-ever-was, wait-for-help, willing-to-settle not-for-profit organizations who can't demonstrate their ability to give a darn and to make a difference.

However, if you deeply and passionately care about making a difference, it's never been easier to connect with and utilize resources of business owners and employees and volunteers to help you accomplish your mission.

But ... it all starts with the not-for-profit leader. It all starts with the small business owner. Can they find each other and are they willing to do the work?

Are you willing to do the work?

What are you prepared to do?

We're waiting ... and we're watching.

97. ANATOMY OF A SMALL RELIEF EFFORT, PART I

In May of 2011, my friends, David and Meghan Rowe, staged a relief effort at their restaurant in Columbia for the tornado victims of Joplin, and they asked for my help. I wanted to chronicle our efforts since we weren't professional event planners. We learned a lot. I'm going to retell the story here in present tense over the next couple chapters in hopes you can learn something, too.

We are collecting hygiene items and bottled water. None of us have done anything like this before. I'm writing stuff down that I learn along the way.

"I want to do something."

That's what David said when my phone rang on Monday morning – fourteen hours after the tornado unleashed hell on Joplin, Missouri.

But we should cut that off before it starts, shouldn't we? It didn't unleash hell on Joplin, exactly. It unleashed hell on the people, pets, homes, hopes and dreams of the southwestern Missouri city. To say the city name alone somehow impersonalizes it.

This is most certainly personal.

David and Meghan wanted to do something. They wanted my help.

None of us are wealthy or famous. We don't have instant access to resources or staff to marshal together a plan even if we could come up with one.

So, I did the only thing I knew how to do: reached out to people smarter than me.

My friend, Sarah Hill, of KOMU TV suggested I reach out to Tim Rich of The Heart of Missouri United Way who suggested I reach out to Peggy Kirkpatrick of The Food Bank For Central & Northeast Missouri.

It was about this time that I smacked myself on the head for not thinking to make Peggy my first call.

When the Mt. Rushmore of central Missouri's erected, you'd be hard-pressed to find a person who wouldn't put Peggy up there.

A whirling dervish of smiles, hugs, common sense and action, Peggy and her Director of Development, Bobbie Kincade, came to our aid yesterday morning.

They recognized two boys who were nice but none-too-bright.

As we (and by "we," I mean Peggy and Bobbie) began to hash out our plan for not only collection but staging and distribution, I started taking notes on the smart stuff Peggy was saying.

It filled four pages.

But, in the awful chance you're faced with having to stage such a relief effort yourself, here are two things Peggy said that stuck with me above all else:

1. **If all you get's a bar of soap and three bucks, you've made a difference.**

People in need can use a bar of soap and three bucks. It's not a competition to see who can raise the most money or gather the most supplies. Every little bit helps. Every. Little. Bit.

2. **Besides first responders efforts, you know when – in a relief effort – help matters most? After Anderson Cooper leaves.**

Once the satellite trucks move on to the next sad story, Joplin will still be in emotional and physical shreds. Are we still willing to help? What's the plan to help in three weeks? Three months? Six months?

So, we're getting back together today to consider and act upon the help Peggy and Bobbie gave us – we're planning out things like signs and chairs and a tent and what to do if people won't be around on Saturday (we have drop off bins at the restaurant now) and if people want to write checks (make them out to "The Food Bank") and how to get out the word.

We don't have a traditional media partner for this event. They're all doing their own thing.

We're just a couple guys with kids who want to be good examples to them by helping the people of Joplin feel just a little bit better and maybe a little cleaner with soap and deodorant and toothpaste and toothbrushes.

So, on Saturday from 8 AM to 2 PM, we'll be in D. Rowe's Parking Lot at Forum & Nifong in Columbia (behind Walgreen's) collecting hygiene supplies & bottled water.

It ain't much in the grand scheme of things, but it's the best we can do.

At least, it is now that we have Peggy helping us.

98. ANATOMY OF A SMALL RELIEF EFFORT, PART 2

As I wrote on Tuesday, my friends, David and Meghan Rowe, are staging a relief effort this Saturday at their restaurant in Columbia for the tornado victims of Joplin, and they asked for my help. We are collecting hygiene items and bottled water. None of us have done anything like this before. I'm writing stuff down that I learn along the way.

This idea was born on a Monday. It's Thursday. Our relief effort – collecting hygiene items and bottled water – is coming together for Saturday in D. Rowe's parking lot in Columbia.

Here are some more things I've learned in the past forty-eight hours:

You can't be afraid to pimp your friends, as long as ... you don't ask for stuff all the time. David and I both try to do a lot of things for people without asking for stuff in return. It's how David got the University of Missouri Football Team involved. It's how I got (my client) Epic Dental's President Donald Bailey to donate more than $1,000 worth of toothpaste.

(By the way, speaking of the Mizzou Football team, the coaches' kids are going to have a lemonade stand at our relief effort Saturday. They wanted to help, too. Isn't that cool?)

We're so blessed to have experts as partners with the capacity to stage and store until Joplin's ready for our help. The Food Bank has drivers ready to go, but reports out of

Joplin indicate they don't have the capacity yet to distribute the supplies we'll collect. Once our partners at The Food Bank get the call, their drivers can deploy at a moment's notice.

After spending just a couple days doing this, I'm in awe of first responders and people who run into the destruction and keep their heads as best they can. If I would have learned this at a younger age, I would have chosen a different profession.

Speaking of awe, Joplin native Brent Beshore and his team have coordinated with The Heart of Missouri United Way to raise hundreds of thousands of dollars in just days. They have a fundraiser tonight (Thursday, May 26) at The Museao building in Columbia. He and his team have done otherworldly things in such a short amount of time. He's done his family and his hometown so proud.

So have so many others. The stories of grace and glory – of semi-trucks and church prayer groups – stream in from across the globe. My client in the UK emailed me this morning to see how we were doing and wondering if there was anything she could do.

The one thing I feel kinda bad about – or rather, I feel bad that I feel bad: I'm sorry, but I've seen several cases of businesses getting on Facebook and saying, "Hey, for each person who likes our page, we'll donate a buck," or "If we get to 800 followers by 3 PM, we'll donate $2,500."

That just leaves me feeling all oily. Am I wrong? Is any donation – even if it kinda sorta appears to be self-serving – a good donation?

I feel bad that I feel bad.

We're all a little gunshy here in Missouri. Yesterday afternoon, in my central part of the state, more than a dozen counties were under tornado warnings at the same time. As our sirens were going off in Columbia, all I could think about was my son – downtown at school, and how we couldn't be there with him.

And, as I sat there feeling helpless, I felt guilty for being so selfish. My son was safe and sound in one of the oldest, most solid brick buildings in Boone County, and he would be fine, and we would probably be fine.

I've learned I don't have problems. I have a few inconveniences here and there, but I don't have any real problems.

This afternoon, David's doing a bunch of media interviews about the effort on Saturday. A local radio group – Cumulus Media – has really reached out to us to help us spread the word even though they have their own efforts they've been conducting.

KOMU-TV has really worked hard to spread the word for us as well. They have a telethon tonight in conjunction with Beshore's event at The Museao building.

Lots of people making things happen. Lots of people doing good deeds. Lots of people realizing their troubles ain't so troubling.

Gotta run. There's work to be done.

99. ANATOMY OF A SMALL RELIEF EFFORT, PART 3

The day has come. For us, the week has gone by fast. We've seen and heard stories of grace and horror.

It's time to do what we're gonna do. I turned onto Club Village Drive from Forum and saw the big honkin' Mizzou Football truck. It was a pretty cool sight.

Cooler still? The fact that people were unloading supplies from their cars, trucks and SUVs, and we had just begun.

We'll be here collecting hygiene items and bottled water under the supervision of The Food Bank For Central & Northeast Missouri until 2 PM today. We have no expectations, and as Peggy from the Food Bank reminded us, "if you get three bucks and a bar of soap, you've made a difference."

Thank you, Peggy. Thank you, everyone.

I started to get a bit of dread yesterday as the Internet buzzed with fears that Joplin had too many supplies like the kind we were collecting. Watching the KOMU/ Museao/United Way telethon on Thursday night (where they raised more than a million dollars – WOW!), I heard one of the anchors say, "They don't need supplies, they need money!"

Ooh. Were we doing the wrong thing?

Then yesterday, a Columbia Tribune reporter I really respect, Janese Silvey, tweeted a message from FEMA that they didn't need more unsolicited supply donations.

I emailed Peggy from the Food Bank and she reassured me by saying these donations aren't unsolicited, and that Joplin was going to need every ounce of help we could provide.

Long after the cameras leave, Joplin's going to need every ounce of help we can provide.

Here, today, at D. Rowe's just north of Forum & Nifong behind Walgreen's, we're so grateful for the leadership The Food Bank has provided us, and we're equally thankful for the support and weight Mizzou Football has thrown behind this.

We hope you can make it by today – even if it's just three bucks and a bar of soap … you're making a difference.

Thank you.

100. ANATOMY OF A SMALL RELIEF EFFORT, PART 4

That truck you saw in the previous chapter? People with big hearts came from all over mid-Missouri Saturday and filled it.

Yep. Full – palettes from front to back.

When we started this on Monday, we didn't know what to expect, but people started lining up shortly after the truck pulled up.

It was heartwarming. It was a little overwhelming. It was even surprising.

We couldn't have done it without The Food Bank For Central & Northeast Missouri guiding us, then staging and storing our collection until time comes to deliver.

We couldn't have done it without Mizzou Football, their volunteers, and their big honkin' semi truck.

We couldn't have done it without hundreds of people giving up part of their holiday weekend to drop off supplies for the victims of Joplin.

But it's only just the beginning. Long after you read this, Joplin will still need our help.

David, Meghan and I have some other ideas on how to continue to help.

That's maybe the greatest thing about volunteering ... it's addictive.

101. HOUSE MONEY, FOUR LITTLE WORDS & THE NIGHT EVERYTHING CHANGED

Yesterday, as I planned my week ahead, I was stressed about the week ahead – a monstrous to-do list as our practice and levels of responsibility continue to grow.

Then, last night, everything changed.

My wife first said the word "autism" to me when our son was thirteen months old. At eighteen months old, he was officially diagnosed with moderate autism. If you're familiar with the disorder, you know it's a wide spectrum. Our son's diagnosis was somewhere out in right-center field.

Non-verbal until about four, life with Will was a daily battle between patience and frustration. Imagine an automatic-drip coffee filter. That was Will's brain. Still is: waaaaay too much sensory input with just a drip at a time coming out.

For more than five years, I've told my son I loved him when I put him to bed.

Last night, for the first time, he said, "I love you, too."

By my count:

I've told my son I loved him as I wished him good night more than 1,500 times.

I've professionally written more than 2,500,000 words over the past fifteen years.

None of them had as much impact on my life as the four he casually offered up last night before closing his eyes.

So, here's the thing. My scary week? Not so scary anymore.

Me? I'm playing on house money for the rest of this week.

Everything else that gets done is just a bonus.

Funny thing is – I woke up ready to go ... fearless ... with nothing so troubling or problematic. I want to get more done.

Why not pretend you're playing on house money today? Be a little bit bolder, a little friendlier, and a little bit more adventurous. Why not?

You know we're all playing on house money, right?

When I shared the news of Will's four words with my friends last night, Cathy shared this:

One of the strange things about living in the world is that it is only now and then one is quite sure one is going to live forever and ever and ever. ~ Frances Hodgson Burnett

Hmm. Here's the other thing, and hopefully what keeps these 600 words from veering too far off course:

It wasn't some miraculous bit of serendipity. These four words came from the patience, frustration, work, sweat, creativity, rewards, tears, and laughter of seven days a week of in-home therapy, and five days a week of additional outside-the-home therapy.

These four words came from practice.

These four words came from work.

For more than five years, I hoped these words would come. Since he was eighteen months old, we've given every available bit of time and money to help them find their way from brain to mouth.

Hope alone ain't a strategy. Perhaps you've heard.

There's your secret then: If you want something badly enough, you'll practice every day and make tiny little bits of progress in the face of staggering cliffs of frustration.

And you just keep coming back like some stubborn stupid fighter that doesn't know when to quit.

You do the hard things. Sometimes those things take five years or more. Patience becomes the greater expression of commitment. Commitment becomes the greater expression of grace.

Easy? You want easy? Great. Enjoy your life of mediocrity.

Hmm. Guess this was a little bit about strategic planning after all.

Thanks, buddy.

UPDATE: Last night, I was met again with silence. That's okay. Baby steps ...

102. GOOD TUESDAYS

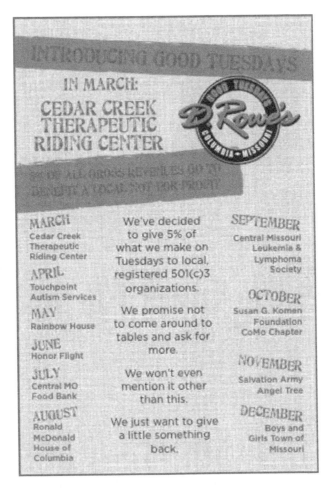

Remember the owners of D. Rowe's from the relief effort story?

I owe a lot to David and Meghan Rowe. David was one of the first people we met when we moved to Columbia in

February of 2003 (and one of the many, many things in my life for which I have to thank Scotty David Cox, right?).

David and Meghan and I have been friends for a long time. We do a little work together here and there. I write some things for them. He feeds me and lets me sit the back of his restaurant and write this book.

Even if he wasn't a cancer survivor, I'm certain David would still have a huge heart. David understands what it takes, and he feels the debt to give back and help others.

One of the ways we found to do good deeds locally is with good Tuesdays.

The program was simple: on Tuesdays, D. Rowe's would quietly give five percent of all gross sales to a local registered 501(c)(3) not-for-profit organization.

The organization changed from month to month but they were all local, and they were all officially registered not-for-profits. This helped prevent (usually well-intentioned) people from trying to get David to raise money to send their kids to space camp or the high school band to the Rose Bowl parade or something.

Notice the language on the sign, though. It's important.

"We don't want to make a big deal of it."

"We're not going to mention it other than this."

David and Meghan didn't want people to feel guilty for *not* giving.

This is a new way of thinking: not trying to make people feel bad about doing something good and not going around from table to table asking for more and making people uncomfortable.

Your company doesn't need one of those giant check thingies or a grand spectacle. When you start to make a difference in your own community, people will know. It's never been easier for people to find out.

Actions have never spoken louder.

103. HOW I QUIT SMOKING

On February 21, 2008, I quit smoking.

It shocked people who knew me. Few believed – including me initially – I could do it. I started when I was eighteen and never looked back.

Of course, quitting saved my life, but it did more. Here's a quick digest of how I did it and what I noticed.

1.   It was my fourth try.

The longest I'd gone smoke-free prior to quitting was thirteen days.

2.   I was no longer around many smokers.

In previous attempts my environment was filled with smokers. It made a huge difference.

3.   I started by specifically counting the number of cigarettes I smoked each day.

I needed a baseline. I always figured I smoked about a pack. Nope. I smoked – almost without fail – thirty a day plus or minus two.

4.   Before I started using medication, I cut down to fifteen per day.

That's still a lot of smokes. I told myself that was still a lot of smokes. It showed me I could cut to half and keep it there for a couple weeks without any help.

5.   I went to see a doctor who prescribed Chantix.

My wife made the appointment, and I got mad at her. Of course I did. I was an addict.

Be prepared for people to say, "Oh, you need drugs to do it, huh? I quit cold turkey."

Those people are self-righteous jerkfaces. Ignore them.

Chantix was great for me. It really did make me enjoy smoking less, and I began to slowly cut back by half again and again until I was done on February 21, 2008. I totally dug the dreams. I couldn't wait to go to sleep at night. But, then …

6.   I also quit drinking for a while.

The two were inexorably linked for me. Smoking's always been tethered to other stuff for me – driving, drinking (though not at the same time) and finishing projects. I've never had an habitual problem drinking to excess, but to this day I find I rarely drink.

7.   I found replacements for those situations.

Straws   worked in the car. I cut 'em in half and worked and worked 'em. I had little half-straws everywhere. I also started drinking lots and lots of water.

I couldn't totally cut coffee but I cut back for a while.

I also would take breaks after finishing projects, but instead of smoking I would breath … oxygen … it's this other drug that's a pretty good high. And it's a lot cheaper.

8.   I told myself – and anyone who would listen – that I was just quitting for the day.

I couldn't do anything about tomorrow. I believe alcoholics anonymous uses this philosophy. It really took the pressure off to not imagine such a big, long time of never smoking again.

For more than six months, I kept my last half-pack of Camels sitting on my office desk. They were there if I wanted them. I just didn't want them. Listen – you're either deciding to quit or not, right? Hiding smokes or throwing away smokes wasn't going to stop me. I would just go buy more if I wanted.

I had two packs in my glove box for two years. Never touched them. Finally threw them away when we sold the car.

9. I ate Skittles.

Don't eat Skittles. I gave up smoking and took up Skittles. Not only is the sugar totally bad for you, but I gained a lot of weight. I have since lost some of it, but I have more to go.

10. I had a great coach.

I enlisted a friend – not my wife – who was both healthy and a non-smoker to encourage me. I was proud when I could call Heidi and say, "Today's another day." She would go bananas for me, and that helped.

That's it.

I only now have the occasional craving when I see lots of smoking in a movie or we go to Vegas. I don't miss it after writing something – that was the biggest thing.

What I like:

I'm more invested in conversations or classes or meetings. I'm not constantly distracted thinking about when I'm going to get my next smoke. We just got back from meetings in Austin where I used to miss close to an hour-and-a-half of the day with my little five or ten minute breaks throughout the day.

I don't stink. My kids don't think I stink. My wife doesn't think I stink. My clothes don't stink. My hair doesn't stink. It's nice.

My sense of smell improved. My colds and coughs aren't as painful.

That said, I've never noticed the whole improved taste thing. Ever.

None of us know when our number's up, but I've drastically increased my chances of sticking around to play with my kids for a significantly longer time.

Summary

If you or someone you love smokes. It can be done. I never thought I would quit. I loved smoking. It was my favorite thing.

No one who knew me thought I would quit, but I did.

Hell yes, it's hard. It's the hardest thing I've ever done.

But there's grace in accomplishing the hard tasks, isn't there?

Since then, nothing seems as difficult.

That might be the biggest benefit of all.

104. OPENING DAY

About a million years ago, I sat at the bar with Scotty and Aric – my two buddies.

That night, for the first time, I said out loud:

"Our son has autism."

I didn't break down in tears when I told them. The tears came about an hour later when it occurred to me – there with my guys – and I muttered aloud:

"I guess he'll never get to play little league."

It's funny the things you focus on as a relatively new dad – the things that you idealize and dream about and consider important.

At that time we had no idea what was in store for our family over the next few years. I guess none of us do.

I could rack up a bazillion baseball metaphors, but I won't.

I will tell you the kid loves baseball. He adores baseball.

And, God bless him, we are fortunate enough to live in a special town with some special people who started a special league for special kids.

We've all come a long way. Him most of all.

About four years later – tonight – I asked my son if it would be okay if I was his coach in the Challenger League of Daniel Boone Little League Baseball.

He looked me in the eye. Unprompted. If you know him, you know that's something, but there's more.

"Yes!" he said.

If you'd like to come cheer on some special kids, look us up on Monday evenings on Diamond 4.

Three innings. Everybody bats. Nobody loses.

Nobody.

Later, after he went to bed, his mama told me what Will told her about me being his coach:

"That … is … exciting! Now, everyone will know he is my dad!"

105. WRITE FOR A LOCAL CHARITY

A writer's most valuable resource is her time.

If you're already a professional writer, I promise you a little bit of you withers with each car ad, with each mercantile pursuit. You may be extremely proud of both the client and the work, yet it happens nonetheless.

Recharge by giving your time to a small, local not-for-profit who has neither the time nor talent nor resources to persuade the community to help them the way you can.

Do it outside your normal working hours. Give when it hurts.

Just pick one. Contact them. Uncover their need and just start helping. They'll be grateful beyond words, and your words will come easily because it's far easier using your wordsmithing powers for selfless good.

Furthermore, for those of you yearning to be professional writers, this will give you the chance to work on your craft for a real, honest-to-goodness business when no one else will give you the chance. Yet.

Imagine one day in the not-too-distant-future how your prospective client will feel when they see your portfolio bursting with emotionally evocative copy for local not-for-profits.

They'll certainly think and feel you're a most remarkable person. And they would be correct.

Go. Write. Make a difference. Unleash grace.

Amen.

106. BLACK HOLES ARE DOORKNOBS, BY WILL MILES

My son wanted to write a chapter. I asked him to give you advice.

Now, to be fair, his typing is still improving, so he shot a video of his advice.

You can see it at www.GoodCompanyStuff.com.

107. GOOD GAME

Photo Courtesy of Jen Lee Reeves

I told my wife last night that coaching the Challenger League baseball team is quickly becoming my favorite ninety minutes of the week.

Girls and boys play together. Everybody bats every inning. We don't keep score.

We have three strict rules on the D. Rowe's Cardinals:

Have fun.

Be safe.

Have fun.

And yet, I can't help but notice – in the massive Daniel Boone Little League Complex – other players and their families on typical teams occasionally walk past field four and point and snicker.

I don't get upset or sad ... much ... anymore. My kids are having a blast, and we've really seen an improvement in their performance since we got HGH testing banned in the most recent collective bargaining agreement.

No, what makes me sad is what I saw last night – a father berating his typical child as they left a different field:

"That was terrible. You've got to try harder. You think this is just a game?"

Dude. Really? Your kid's ten.

Then, I get home and see this on Facebook from my friend Dulsey:

So tonight at Danny's soccer game (He is three, by the way) some jackass father told the crowd that he informed his son to "punch the kid in the nose if he keeps pushing you down." I almost lost it. They are three years old.

Dear parents trying to re-live your lost childhood:

Stop being poopheads.

I won't say either father was acting retarded – a word I heard last week from a passerby. That would be an insult to Camryn, a wonderful young lady on my team with Down syndrome.

She way outclasses you two, and she clearly has a better head on her shoulders.

My wife nailed it last night when I was talking to her about parents and seriousness and absurdity.

"It reminds me of *Toddlers and Tiaras*. That's it!" she said, "It's like beauty pageants for boys."

All kids are special. All kids have the right to play games and be happy.

All kids have a right to be applauded.

You know the best moment of our game last night?

Gregory.

Last week, our first week, Gregory brought two new batting gloves that he couldn't wait to show me. He adored these things. He got into a pushing argument in week one with another boy on our team who thought they were really cool and wanted to touch them.

Last night, our second week, I watch Andrew – the second boy – coming up to bat wearing one of those gloves. I looked at Gregory, and he smiled the proudest smile you'll ever see.

Winning. Duh.

You think this is a game?

It is, and it's a good game.

Photo Courtesy of Jen Lee Reeves

108. DEFAULTING ON LIFE

Want a more stimulating, less anxious, more satisfying week?

Want to wake up Saturday morning feeling refreshed and content?

You remember contentment, don't you?

We've gotten so busy we've managed to get our priorities out of whack again, but it didn't happen overnight.

It crept up on us slowly and quietly.

The grind is a ninja.

More and more, it seems we say "no" by default to things in our family life.

Sorry, I really don't have time to take you to soccer practice. Mama can do it.

No, I really don't have the energy to stay up and talk tonight. Can't we just watch TV?

I wish I could, son, but daddy's too busy right now.

Stop me if you've heard those.

We find time for work, extra work, work-related community service, networking and busy work.

We say "yes" by default to work stuff.

Switch the default boxes.

This week, try and find ways to say "yes" to family stuff.

Family, extra family, family-related community service, netfamilying and busy family.

And turn on "no" by default to work stuff.

Are you afraid they'll fire you?

Do you really want to work for jerkfaces like that?

Just asking.

I'm going to go play with Will and Sarah now.

ABOUT THE AUTHOR

Part Dave Barry, Part Dave Ramsey, Part that Dave guy from the movie, uhh, *Dave*, Tim Miles uses common sense, kindness and an unquenchable curiosity to meet force with force - helping people (willing to do the work) to be successful.

Tim started creating advertising campaigns in 1995. In the ten years that followed, he won more than eighty awards for his ideas and execution of those ideas. He's worked with hundreds of small businesses all over the world.

When their son was diagnosed with autism November 21, 2005, Tim learned pretty much everything he thought he knew was wrong, and he's made it his mission since to teach people to look at the world a little differently and separate the merely urgent from the truly important.

Tim's paying clients help to subsidize his volunteer and fundraising efforts with more than a dozen small not-for-profit organizations. In the last five years, he's been fortunate to speak to more than a thousand not-for-profit organizations about how there's never been a better time to do what it is they do, but there's never been a more important time to be good at what it is they do.

As founder and head custodian for The Imagination Advisory Group, Tim consults businesses in four countries and regularly speaks to companies, conferences, and colleges about how to communicate more powerfully, how to do just a little bit more with a little bit less, and how best to let the world see you as you really are ... not as you think you should be.

He married Deidre - who's much smarter and infinitely better looking than he deserves. This is not hyperbole. Ask anyone who knows them both. They have two children, Will and Sarah, and live out in the country on a couple acres in the middle of the Midwest with Kitty and Fish44.

Tim chronicles mistakes made, lessons learned, and the sordid misadventures and hijinks of clients, friends, and family at www.TheDailyBlur.com.